D0873892

1502

THE STORY OF SAN FRANCISCO

THE STORY

OF

SAN FRANCISCO

---- ★ ----

by CHARLOTTE JACKSON

Illustrated by KURT WERTH

Landmark
BOOKS

RANDOM HOUSE · NEW YORK

For Matthew Bell Skinner

CONTENTS

THE STORY OF SAN FRANCISCO

1 THE PORT OF SAN FRANCISCO

Just fifty years after Christopher Columbus landed in the West Indies and raised the Spanish flag, Juan Rodriguez Cabrillo dropped anchor outside the portals of San Francisco Bay and claimed all of California for Spain. It was easy to miss the entrance to the landlocked harbor because most of the year it was hidden by a thick curtain of fog and mist.

In the year 1579 Francis Drake, the bold English sea captain, came close to the entrance. But
he missed the rough gateway of water and sailed
on to find safe anchorage in a small harbor that
some of the early navigators had misnamed Puerto
de San Francisco.

During their stay, Drake and his sailors made
friends with the Indians, and the friendly red men
took the Englishmen on several trips into the surrounding country. The Indians told the white men
many legends of the new country and were eager
to lead them over the rough hills to a larger body
of water which lay farther south.

Drake, impatient to get back to England,
wouldn't explore farther. He claimed the land for
England and sailed across the Pacific. When he
completed his trip around the world and reached
England, he reported to Queen Elizabeth that he
had claimed a new land for England. The Queen
was so pleased that she made him a knight.

In those ancient days events happened slowly.
It was almost two hundred years later that Gaspar
de Portolá, a soldier of Spain, was sent on an
overland expedition from San Diego to Monterey,
which was Spain's northernmost port in California
at that time.

The little band of Spaniards and Indians marched over rough country, high hills and hot deserts all during the summer months. It wasn't until October that, tired and footsore, they came to a range of hills overlooking the Pacific Ocean. Evidently they had missed the port of Monterey for these landmarks were not the ones that showed on their maps.

Portolá sent some of his men to hunt for game in the hills. One of the men came back and reported seeing a large inland body of water that stretched for miles to the northeast.

Next morning Portolá sent this hunter and his own trusted sergeant, José Ortega, with some of the other men to see if they could find the water the hunter had seen from the hilltop.

The men found the water and walked along its edge until they came to the high cliff that was one of the portals guarding the landlocked harbor. They had come much farther north than Monterey. Clearly this northern harbor was an important one for Spain to have.

When news of Portolá's discovery got to the King of Spain, the King knew that he must claim the port as soon as possible. Otherwise the English or Dutch might get a foothold in California.

He ordered an adventurous young sea captain, Juan Manuel de Ayala, to sail to the new port and survey the waters for Spain.

It was a slow, hard trip. Not until August 5, 1775, did Captain Ayala see the entrance to the port. With darkness coming on and with a strong flood tide his ship, the *San Carlos*, made its way through the unknown passage between the high rugged cliffs.

Finally at half-past ten at night, the *San Carlos* anchored on the north shore of the bay near the banks of what is now Sausalito. It was the first ship to cast anchor in San Francisco Bay.

Captain Ayala stayed on for a month, making a complete survey of the bay and the surrounding territory. He named the wooded green island in the middle of the bay "*Nuestra Señora de los Angeles*," "Angel Island." In his report to his country he said that the "port was not one but many, with but a single entrance." His work was finished by the first week in September, and he sailed for Monterey and thence back to New Spain.

2   OVER DESERT SANDS AND MOUNTAINS

The year before, the King of Spain had received a report from Mexico about a trail-blazing expedition by a young captain in the army, Juan Bautista de Anza.

Captain Anza had heard of the unsuccessful attempts of many ships to land on the northern coast. He wanted to break a trail northward over mountains and deserts to the northern outpost.

Spain's viceroy in Mexico City listened to the enthusiastic young man and was persuaded to let him find a land route over the mountains and the desert.

Anza assembled a band of thirty-four men with one hundred and forty horses and sixty-five head of cattle. They set out in January in 1774. Early in April, they had reached the mission at Monterey. There Captain Anza decided not to go on to the port of San Francisco but returned to Mexico.

The Spanish viceroy lost no time in sending an account of Captain Anza's trail blazing to the King of Spain. When the King replied, his orders were to equip an expedition as soon as possible. This time families and all their possessions were to take the new trail to the northern Spanish outpost. Captain Anza was asked to head the expedition and was given the title of colonel. The hardy, brave men who had accompanied him on the first journey were to go along too, and for this they were awarded pensions for life.

This new expedition was for colonization and would have many more people than the first. Colonel Anza at once chose a good priest to accompany him, Father Pedro Font.

Each family who made the journey would be given a fresh grant of land of many leagues that would be theirs and their families' forever. One hundred seventy-six men and women accompanied Anza on his journey. The party included a goodly body of soldiers equipped in deerskin and carrying broadswords. There were also forty muleteers to take charge of the pack animals, mules laden with the household goods, ammunition and food. Bright glass beads and tobacco were stored in the saddlebags, too, for trade with the Indians along the way. Forty *vaqueros*, or cowboys, went along to ride herd on the three hundred head of cattle. Also there were horses enough for everyone to ride and a herd of them besides.

Finally, on September 29, 1775, this historic pilgrimage was ready to start.

Friends left behind wistfully watched the unwieldy caravan get under way. Colonel Anza and his officers and soldiers led the procession. Father Font rode behind the soldiers, at the head of the band of women and children. Then came the mules with their heavy loads, prodded along by the drivers.

The first part of the journey was fairly easy. But Anza knew the most hazardous part of the journey would be the crossing of the great deserts, with the vast areas between water holes and fields of grass for the animals.

The weeks that followed were ones of terrible hardship. Fresh food became scarce, and water dribbling from desert wells seemed just a trickle. Sometimes the whole company waited for two and three days while scouts went ahead to locate other water holes.

After many days' marching, the company came to the land of the Yuma tribe. These Indians proved friendly and gave generously from their stores of food. They brought fresh melons, too, and several of the sick, whose lives were feared for, got well in a few days from the fresh diet.

The first part of December the party got under way once more, their saddlebags packed with as much fresh food as they could tuck away.

Now the trail was through the treeless desert. Its biting winter winds whipped the coarse sand into the faces of the animals, making them plunge wildly to get a foothold in the shifting earth. The people covered their faces with shawls and kerchiefs. They pushed on with their heads lowered against the never-ceasing wind.

Colonel Anza rode on ahead of the caravan and sometimes would be gone for days seeking new water holes. Then he would gallop back to encourage his people and comfort the children. He was a good leader and father to his people, and the pilgrims never lost faith on the whole painful journey across the desert.

On Christmas Day the party camped on the edge of the great desert, near a spring in the rocky country, and gave thanks for their safe journey so far. There was a celebration, with campfires of dry mesquite blazing high, and singing and dancing until the morning.

Colonel Anza encouraged his people by telling them that the worst part of the journey was over. Now the crossing of the mountains would bring them to the fertile California valleys, and there would be no more hardships for them.

The party reached the San Gorgonio Pass the first week of the new year in the midst of a bitter hail- and snowstorm. This was their first encounter with such weather. The people were terrified and huddled together, almost freezing, to wait for it to pass. The storm did die, but with its dying came a trembling of the earth and a terrifying rumble under the earth that made the frightened people think that now surely their end had come.

Then after a painful climb through the mountain pass, the colonists came to a wide, fertile valley with trees and grass glistening in yellow sunlight.

The trip through the valley was a joyful one.

Colonel Anza's party almost froze in the snowstorm.

At the San Gabriel mission they stopped for a month's rest before pressing northward.

The next part of the march was pleasant, too, in the balmy spring weather and through the level valleys. The very line of march that the caravan took is the same one used today. The colonists crossed the *Rio de Monterey*, now called the Salinas River. Finally, on the tenth of March, they arrived at Monterey, then the most important port in California. Father Junipero Serra came from nearby Mission San Carlos to welcome the weary travelers and extend the hospitality of the Mission to them.

While the party rested there, Colonel Anza with Father Font and ten of his ablest men started off on horseback for the port of San Francisco. They took provisions for twenty days.

It was the middle of March when they journeyed along the coastline toward the north. On March twenty-seventh, they encamped on a small lake near the shore of the bay they had finally reached. They were on a little creek, where there was plenty of pasturage for the animals. Then Colonel Anza went about laying out the village. His men explored the eastern side of the bay and as far north and west as they could go. For the presidio, or fort, he chose the flat headland overlooking the steep cliffs at the entrance to the harbor. There guns could be easily trained on enemy ships trying to enter the bay. Wisely he chose the flat pasture lands farther south for the mission buildings.

When Colonel Anza returned to Monterey after laying out the village, he found a message from the viceroy. It told him to hasten home to Mexico City. So the brave leader with Father Font left almost at once and neither man had the satisfaction of leading the settlers to the new land after all.

To his faithful lieutenant, Joseph Joachim Moraga, Anza gave the job of leading the colonists the sixty-odd miles to the new settlement.

The comparatively short march from Monterey to the site of their new home was a delightful excursion compared to the terrors the pilgrims had experienced on the Colorado desert. On the twenty-seventh of June the expedition arrived at the lagoon at the tip of the bay, where they paused and built a crude chapel of rushes and branches for the saying of mass.

On the second day, a feast day in the church, Father Palou said the first mass on the site of San Francisco. This was just eight months after the colonists started their long journey across the cruel desert to their new home. They all sang thanks for their safe deliverance. This was on June 29, 1776, just five days before our American Fathers signed the Declaration of Independence from England at Independence Hall in Philadelphia.

3 THE PRESIDIO AND THE MISSION

For a month the settlers remained in their makeshift camp awaiting the arrival of the schooner
San Carlos from Monterey. It was to bring much-
needed supplies and artisans to build the presidio
and the mission buildings. The ship, leaving
Monterey a few days after the departure of the
colonists, had been delayed by strong winds and

did not enter the port until the middle of August.

While waiting for the ship to arrive, Moraga had his men cut timber for the building of the presidio. The people became restless during that long month. Food was growing short and their clothes, warm enough for the gentle climate of Mexico, were not enough to keep out the chill winds of the Pacific Ocean or to keep them dry during the nights of heavy fog.

The Indians, so friendly at first, became bolder on seeing how defenseless the settlers really were.

The *San Carlos* finally entered the port and anchored just inside the cliffs near where the presidio was to be built. The ship was unloaded as speedily as possible. The sailors from the *San Carlos*, as well as the carpenters they brought with them, helped the settlers in laying out and building the new presidio, a good warehouse for provisions, the commander's house and the chapel. The soldiers built their own houses under the direction of the captain of the post.

Work went very quickly on the buildings with no rain to hinder the workmen. By September the soldiers had completed their log houses with flat thatched roofs. The government house was ready soon afterward. The warehouse was built and filled

With great ceremony, they took over the new presidio.

with supplies that had come in the *San Carlos*.
Most of the mission buildings were finished, too,
and a central plaza was laid out in the village.

With impressive ceremony, formal possession of
the presidio took place on the seventeenth of September. It was a cloudless fall day. The people
could see for miles across the blue Pacific from
the presidio site. Down below the white cliffs, the
little ship *San Carlos* was anchored in the choppy
water of the bay.

Right after the ceremony, the two commanders,

The little ship San Carlos *was anchored in the bay.*

one from the presidio and one from the *San Carlos*, left with a party to explore the rivers that fed the bay and the surrounding land to the east. The men from the ship went by launch. The commander of the presidio and his men went on horseback around the south end of the bay. Both parties agreed to meet at the mouth of the rivers.

After two days' sailing the men in the launch found that the harbor had no opening to the sea except the one they had left—the wide gate between the two great cliffs.

The land expedition, when it started out, crossed a low range of hills and found itself on a vast plain cut by a wide river.

After a summer in their fog-swept village on the bay, the dry heat of the valley was very welcome. The men found the river shallow enough for pleasant bathing. They saw groves of oaks and willows that marked the course of waterways all about them in the flat distances. Beyond they saw high mountains with snow-covered peaks. Although some of the men were eager to go farther into the beautiful new land, they retraced their steps along the same trail to their new home on the foggy coast of Puerto de San Francisco. These were the first white men to travel into the vast inner valleys of California.

After the return of both parties of explorers there was another celebration. More mission buildings had been finished. The commander had allowed soldiers from the presidio to help. With Indians to mix the adobe for the walls and cut the rushes for the flat roofs, there was a building, thirty feet long and ten feet wide, with wooden frame covered with clay and a roof of tule reeds. The church was almost as large and adorned with cloths and draperies and banners from the *San Carlos*.

For this celebration the swivel guns were brought ashore from the ship. The soldiers sent salvos from their muskets booming over the water and shot countless rockets into the air.

4 THE VILLAGE OF YERBA BUENA

After Spain had been successful in establishing the
handful of colonists in the bleak outpost on the
shores of San Francisco Bay, she seemed content
to forget her new foothold in California. Monterey
was still the most important port on the coast.
The only ships that entered San Francisco Bay

were occasional ones from Mexico bringing critical supplies to the settlers.

The new village was called Yerba Buena, named for the sweet-smelling herb that blanketed the hillsides. The hills were thickly covered with oaks and pines, too, to the very edge of the sandy shore. In the woods roamed deer, bear, antelope, elk and the dangerous puma. The people found that the fog-drenched land yielded scant crops for their increasing herds, and they asked for larger grants of land to the south and east. In these they planted olive groves, vineyards and fig trees, as well as fields of wheat and barley.

The mission fathers taught the Indians how to till the soil and care for the flocks. The Indians, in turn, showed the settlers how to take the fish from the waters of the bay and how to snare the thickly furred otters and then quickly tap them on the head with an oar and get their skin for warm cloaks to protect them from the fog and cold.

It wasn't such an idyllic life as was the life at the San Gabriel mission that the settlers had visited on the way. The soldiers at the presidio were an idle lot, content with doing nothing. The mission fathers, though, worked hard to teach the settlers how to get the most from the soil and how to spin wool from the sheep and weave it into blankets and clothing.

During the next twenty years the flocks, left to roam, increased tremendously and were slaughtered by the thousand for food. Meat was the chief food of the people, that and a thick pancake called *tortilla*. The killing of the cattle was a very wasteful procedure. The tender fillet was cut out with one slash of the knife, to be broiled over hot coals, while the rest of the carcass was left to rot where it had fallen. It didn't seem to bother the men that they were throwing away valuable hides that could be made into boots and saddles. They were content to wait long periods for their boots and saddles to be brought from the mother country twice a year, or to wear the soft moccasins that the Indians fashioned.

During the autumn months when the weather was warmer than at any other time of the year, the people enjoyed the out-of-doors. They would ride long distances on horseback away from the port to ranches where celebrations would sometimes last for days or weeks at a time. These fiestas were very gay affairs, with guitar music and singing and dancing.

Without protest the men of Yerba Buena watched the strangers haul seal and otter into their boats.

In the village the people often gathered to watch the cruel spectacle of a bear and a bull fighting in the plaza. They would watch until one or the other animal was dead.

During the winter on the Atlantic seaboard, the winds were icy and snow drifted high. But on San Francisco Bay the weather was mild during most of the year. There were fogs and mists and gusty winds, but it was never freezing cold. The adobe houses with their thatched roofs and pounded earthen floors kept out the extreme chill during the cold season, and the thick walls kept the rooms cool during the short season of hot sun.

Until the early 1800's no ships entered the bay except the ones the Spanish government sent with supplies for the settlers. There was no communication with any other part of the world. Spain had settled her port and then forgotten it.

About this time, however, the Yankee clippers from Boston, on their way to and from China and Manila, found that the waters outside the port of San Francisco were thick with sea otter and seals. The hardy American sailors paused here on the way around Cape Horn and slaughtered the otters for their thick fur, which brought them sixty dollars a skin in China where they were made into rich cloaks. The seals were killed for the fine blubber that made oil for the Orient as well as for the people of New England.

The people of Yerba Buena were unaware of this marauding until the seamen, becoming bolder, sent their longboats through the gate of the seaport and into the harbor seeking the fur-bearing and oil-bearing animals. Even then the men of Yerba Buena paid little attention and they would sit idly on the shore and watch the strangers haul their booty into the boats without protest.

The people of the colony were forbidden by law to trade with the outside world, but still a great deal of smuggling went on. The sea captains, seeing how poorly clad the villagers were, would barter with them hides for boots, cotton cloth and woolen garments and knives and kettles. Finally word got back to the Spanish government that illegal trade was going on between the traders and the colonists. Still Spain did nothing about it, and the trading went on.

By this time the Russians from the North were gradually coming down from Alaska with an eye on the rich furs of the otter. The villagers weren't as interested in these ships as were the mission fathers. The fathers were eager to have fine linen for their altars and gold and silver brocades for their vestments. The Russians could supply all these as well as casks for wine, shears for shearing, church bells, and trinkets for the ladies.

The fathers realized that they could barter the hides of the cattle with the Russians for these luxuries, so no longer did they allow the Spaniards to let their cattle rot where they had fallen, but persuaded them to skin the beasts and cure the hides for trade with the foreigners.

The smart Yankee traders soon followed the Russians and sailed boldly into the bay to trade. They would buy the hides for two dollars apiece from the colonists, and sail all the way around South America to Boston. The next year they would return with boots made of the California hides to trade back again to the colonists for more raw hides.

The colonists were always eager to see a Yankee clipper entering the bay. The Americans brought cashmere shawls, Chinese silks, flowered calico, fine perfume and beautiful kerchiefs for the ladies, who thought these Americans were silly to exchange such beautiful objects for the stiff, smelly hides of the range cattle. The men were always glad to find kegs of nails, gunpowder, knives and blankets. Everybody ignored the no-trade laws.

At this time the low adobe houses took on a new grace, thanks to the ships that had come into the harbor. Gay draperies hung on the mud walls and thick rugs lay upon the earthen floors. In the cupboards glistened crystal cups and bowls and red and blue flowered porcelain instead of the clay dishes brought from Mexico.

Late in 1805 the Russians, who had long eyed the California coast with favor, sent one of their ablest sea captains, Rezanov, with a shipload of food to their outpost, Sitka, off the shores of Alaska. He determined to go farther south and see what he could possibly find in California in the way of Russian trading posts and supplies.

He sailed into the bay of San Francisco in April, 1806, and went at once to the presidio to confer with the *comandante*, José Arguello. The *comandante* happened to be in Monterey conferring with the governor, so his son, Luis Arguello, was in charge of the fort.

Young Luis was greatly impressed with entertaining such a fine gentleman from faraway Russia, but was a bit fearful, too, of what his father would do when he returned, for Luis had given Rezanov and his men the freedom of the port. Even young Luis realized that it would take only a glance from the visitor to see how poorly equipped the presidio really was, and how few soldiers Spain had at Yerba Buena.

Rezanov, though, was such a great diplomat that with his charming ways he won even the senior Arguello when he returned from Monterey. In fact everybody in the whole village was hypnotized by the stranger.

The Russian knew that petty officials in a small outpost couldn't sign any treaties but would have to send word to Spain to get permission for any kind of trade agreement. He couldn't help seeing, too, what a fine acquisition California would be for his country. Still, being a diplomat, he knew how to move slowly.

Meanwhile he showered the people with gifts from Japan and other ports. He gave the priest at the mission cloth of gold for vestments and heavy linen for altar cloths. There were silk and woolen shawls for ladies of both high and low rank. Cloth he gave, too, for soldiers' uniforms and fine broadcloth for officers and dons. Toys for the children and even trinkets for the mission Indians he graciously distributed. No one was left out, not even the lowliest sheepherder.

It was only when the handsome Rezanov met the beautiful daughter of the *comandante*, José

Arguello, that his plans for conquest were not uppermost in his thoughts. Concepcion Arguello, a dark-eyed girl of sixteen, was the most beautiful and gracious girl in the whole village. Rezanov fell in love with her at the very first meeting. When he went to Concepcion's father to ask for her hand, Arguello refused at first and told Rezanov of the many difficulties that stood in the way. First, there was the church. Concepcion was a member of the Roman Catholic Church while Rezanov belonged to the Greek Orthodox Church. Then, too, the Arguellos didn't like the idea of their only daughter sailing away to the far north with the Russian captain, perhaps never to return.

Rezanov, though, still the diplomat, was able to persuade her parents that he would concede many things in order to win the fair Concepcion. He was thinking, too, of a friendly alliance between the two countries if he should succeed in marrying the California girl. He knew, of course, that it would be far easier for Russia to settle on the California coast if there was a connection with one of the leading families.

There was no doubt that he was very much in love, but still he was thinking of Russia, too. Finally he told Concepcion's father that he would

After weeks of feasting, Rezanov sailed for Russia.

sail back to his country to obtain permission from his Czar, and then he would go to Rome and seek permission from the Pope for the marriage. It would take all of two years for the journey. To this the Arguello family agreed and the betrothal was announced. After weeks of feasting and dancing, Rezanov sailed away, his ship bulging with grain, hides and furs from the generous Californians.

He did not return, however. After more than thirty years the word came back to Concepcion that her betrothed had perished on the icy steppes of Siberia in his haste to get to St. Petersburg.

Rezanov's death kept the Russians from realizing their grand plans for colonizing the new land. They did succeed in buying a few thousand acres from the Indians north of Yerba Buena at Bodega Bay. Later they built a fort which they called Fort Ross.

The Russian people who came to Fort Ross worked far harder than the Spanish. They had better plows with which to till the soil and better tools of all kinds, that they had brought from home. They planted grain and fruits and vegetables, and lived very comfortably. They brought Indians from the far north who knew how to use kayaks in the rough waters. These Indians managed to slaughter otters by the thousand for their masters to cure and sell in the Orient.

Governor José Arguello dutifully reported the goings on to Mexico City, but he received no reply. For ten years while Mexico was fighting for her independence from Spain, not one Spanish ship with supplies came to the rescue of the colonists. They were completely cut off from the mother country and had to get along as best they could.

This encouraged agriculture, especially in the

outlying missions, Santa Clara to the south and San Rafael across the bay to the north. A brisk trade sprang up between the missions. Barges and canoes, manned by Indians, constantly came into the bay from its tributaries. They brought grain, meat and fruit to the people of Yerba Buena. Occasionally a Yankee ship would come, too, and the people eagerly bartered their hides and beef tallow for clothes and equipment. Still these years were lean ones for the colonists so far away from their mother country.

Now a change came. For over three hundred years Mexico and California had belonged to Spain and been called New Spain. In 1821, after a long bloody war, Mexico at last got her independence from the mother country.

By the fall of 1822 the news of the Mexican independence got to Yerba Buena. California was now a part of independent Mexico. A ship came to Monterey flying the new red, white and green flag instead of the old red and gold colors of Spain. Word was quickly sent by horsemen to the northern port. The old flag was pulled down, and the new colors flew at the presidio and the plaza.

The people were told that they could elect their own governor, and they elected Luis Arguello, brother of Concepcion, the beautiful girl who had been betrothed to Rezanov. Arguello was born in California and understood the new country far better than any man from Mexico did. The first thing he did was to open the ports of California for foreign trade.

5   THE NEW CITIZENS

For a while the people of Yerba Buena couldn't
see much difference in being under the Mexican
flag instead of the flag of Spain. They were so
far removed from the capital that at first there
were few changes. Some of the older settlers,
though, felt sad at being cut off from Spain, which
had ruled gloriously so much of the world for so

long. The younger men were glad that they would no longer have to trade secretly with foreign ships but could do it openly.

Now ships, chiefly American, made regular trips the long way round South America to the open port, seeking whales which were plentiful on the West Coast. These ships anchored in small coves in the bay where the sailors would kill the huge beasts and tie them to the ship. It was the sailor's task to cut off the thick layer of fat blubber just under the skin of the whale and boil it down for oil. The oil was stored in huge barrels and in the holds of the ships and then taken home to burn in lamps. It was very hard work and dangerous, too. Sometimes the ships would be gone from their home port for two or three years.

Some of the sailors became discouraged with the hard work and left their ships to settle in Yerba Buena and the countryside near by. They married Spanish girls and settled down in the new land.

A British whaler came into the port about this time. It was called the *Orion*. A mate on the vessel was a man named William A. Richardson. He was so delighted with the new country that when his vessel sailed away, he stayed behind. He officially became a citizen of Yerba Buena and married a young woman of Spanish blood. This young man was very enterprising and built the first wooden building in the village. This he used as a trading post. It wasn't a very handsome building, just pine boards with canvas stretched between the boards for walls, but it was the first building erected that wasn't made of adobe and tule reeds.

Richardson was also granted by the Spaniards a great deal of land on the northern point of the bay, where there was a deep cove safe for anchorage. This land was called *Rancho Saucelito*, which means "ranch of the willows." Today that cove is called Richardson's Bay, and the grant of land is the pleasantly wooded, hilly town of Sausalito.

Having been a sailor for so many years, Richardson knew how sailors longed for fresh food after drinking brackish water and eating salt meat and fish for long months at sea. Wisely he stocked his store with all the fresh fruits, vegetables, meat and game that he could get when whalers were in port. There were now four more flourishing missions that he could call upon for produce for his trading post. He also had agreements with *rancheros* whose holdings by now stretched for miles along the fingers of the bay and along the fertile river banks into the valleys. From all these places came the fresh food he needed to supply the ships. When ships were in port, crude two-wheeled wooden carts would creak along the rutted roads, stacked with stiff cow hides which always brought two dollars apiece in trade or gold.

Richardson's store was a gay gathering place for sailors, and the villagers as well on market days. After a couple of days in the village, the *rancheros* and mission Indians would go home, their canoes and barges loaded with household goods and clothes that had come the long way around Cape Horn from Boston.

They chose finery for their wives and daughters, too: gaily sprigged calico, warm woolen cloaks, embroidered petticoats and even silk stockings. The Yankee traders brought to William Richardson's store chocolate, which the Spanish relished, and fine canisters of tea from far-off China.

The *rancheros* prized the black iron kettles, huge pots that the sailors used on board ship to boil down the whale blubber. They used them for melting the fat from the cattle. This fat the *rancheros* found brought a fine price at Richard-

Sailors and villagers came to Richardson's store.

son's store when solid pieces were sewn neatly into a steer's hide that could be stowed in the hold of a ship.

Then, again, the indolent Spanish bought candles made of the selfsame tallow the next time the traders came into port with boxes of tallow candles made in Boston.

6   THE OLD SETTLERS ARE UNEASY

During the 1830's all the missions of California were transferred from church rule to the rule of the state. The Franciscan fathers were no longer in charge, and their good work with the Indians deteriorated very rapidly. The missions quickly went into decay.

In 1834 the village of Yerba Buena received

word from the capital in Mexico City that it was to form its own civil government. Elections were held in December and officers were chosen. Francisco de Haro was chosen for the *alcalde*, or chief ruling officer. By January the new local government began to function. The first move of the new government was to give portions of the mission lands to the Indians. The rest of it the officials took for colonization and support of the schools and churches and for the cost of the new government.

The Indians, unused to this new freedom, were at the mercy of the unscrupulous politicians. They lost their lands very soon, gambled, drank to excess, and died by the thousand.

People in the other settlements to the south began to speculate about the opportunities in the raw settlement of Yerba Buena. Among these was an American who lived in the southern pueblo of La Reina de los Angeles (Los Angeles). His name was Jacob Leese. Leese made his way north, first stopping to discuss his plans with his friends, Captain William Hinckley and Nathan Spear, Americans who were in business in Monterey. The three men decided to form a partnership and start a business in Yerba Buena.

Jacob Leese got the governor, Chico, to grant him a good plot of ground in Yerba Buena. He quickly built himself a trading post near the water where he could conduct business with the traders. This was the second structure built by a foreigner in the village.

In the early summer when it was completed, Jacob Leese sent out invitations to all the villagers and others for miles around to a party in honor of the opening of his trading post. He made it a Fourth of July celebration, too, and the Stars and Stripes were raised for the first time in the village.

It was a gay party, with feasting and dancing for three days and presents for all the guests. All the families from the village, as well as people from the faraway *ranchos*, came to the party. They came by oxcart, on horseback, and those from the north shore were ferried across the water in schooners. Captain Hinckley came in his ship, the *Don Quixote*, sailing it up the coast from Monterey. He brought his ship's orchestra to play for the dancing. The fife and drum corps from the presidio came, too.

California families were large. Sometimes there were as many as twenty children in one family.

So, when Jacob Leese gave his party, the trading post was crowded with many young people, all eager to dance to the gay music.

For the three nights of the party the mothers and fathers sat on benches against the rough wooden walls of the store and watched their young people weave back and forth in the intricate figures of the dance. On the third day Jacob Leese invited everybody to ride to a point south of town for a picnic. Here whole sheep and oxen were roasted over live coals and there were horse races and cockfights to entertain the guests.

Jacob Leese's housewarming was the most famous party since the departure of Rezanov. The three Yankees so won the hearts of the settlers that for months to come no one discussed anything but the wonderful fiesta of Jacob Leese.

By this time the original settlers who had come with Colonel Anza were getting old and dying off. Their children were men and women now in the community, but they had the same temperament as their parents. They were easy-going, pleasant, indolent people. Gradually as the new immigrants arrived, the Spaniards receded into the background, content to live their easy lives, with Indian servants to do the hard work.

Horse races and cockfights entertained the guests.

The new settlers, with a sharp eye on the possibilities of the excellent landlocked harbor and the fruitful land about them, were different. These men saw the great possibilities for world trade. Year after year, more and more ambitious men arrived in Yerba Buena. The Swiss, the French, the English and the Dutch came to see what opportunities were offered in the new land. Most of them stayed. They opened shops of all kinds. Blacksmith shops, butcher shops, dress emporiums and saloons were dotted along the muddy main thoroughfare near the water front.

At this period the Spanish influence was diminishing. The women saw that their daughters met the ambitious young men who were constantly arriving. The Anglo-Saxons didn't need much persuading to fall in love with the Spanish beauties. As soon as they married, they became citizens of California and received large grants of land from the government. It was an ideal situation for an ambitious young man to get the girl of his choice plus a large gift of fruitful land.

The old families enjoyed watching the growth of the village and the arrival of all the new people on their shores. They felt a part of it, too, with their daughters married to Yankees and Englishmen.

But the idle times, the easy way of life, were gradually on the wane. More new, ambitious people were arriving each day. Some came by boat. But some were tough mountain men from over the high Sierra—the trappers for furs and scouts. The old settlers, uneasy for the first time, listened to their tales and wondered.

7 THE GRINGOS COME

By this time the word of an ice-free port on the West Coast of the large new continent had got to adventurous people all over the world. They listened to the tales of seamen about the easy life where game and food were plentiful all year. Soon San Francisco Bay was filled with ships from Holland, England, France and even the large southern continent of Australia. Americans, too, came in great numbers from the eastern coast of the country.

In 1837 a young graduate of Harvard College arrived. His name was John Marsh. He had been a schoolteacher and also an Indian agent in the Sioux country, but he was really a fugitive from the government when he arrived. He had been selling firearms to the Indians, which was against the law. He tried to persuade the Californians that a degree from Harvard College was the same as a medical degree and that he was entitled to act as a doctor. He had to leave southern California for doing this and arrived finally at Yerba Buena. Here he worked with Jacob Leese in his trading post for a while and tried to get land from the Mexican government for nothing. He finally bought a large *rancho* from a Californian. It was about thirty miles from the port, at the foot of Mt. Diablo.

Soon after this, another man arrived in Puerto de San Francisco, who was to carve himself an empire in the new land. His name was John Augustus Sutter, and he came on the English brig *Clementine* by way of the Hawaiian Islands. With him he brought ten Kanakas (natives of the Hawaiian Islands), four sailors and a brass cannon. Sutter was a citizen of Switzerland and had come with plenty of money to establish himself in the new land. He was a well-educated man with a pleasant manner, and soon made friends with Jacob Leese and other traders in the village. He hired boats and barges and loaded them with supplies and sailed up the waters of the bay and along the Sacramento River for many miles to the place that is now Sacramento. He told people that he planned a trading post for furs, and wanted fruitful farm lands in the fertile valley at the mouth of the river. He settled a hundred miles from the port, and established a town, a fort, and a huge trading post. Besides he planted hundreds of acres in grain and fruit trees along the banks of the river. The Indians worked for him for very little, and soon he was as rich as a king in the Europe he had left.

John Marsh, the adventurer and fugitive, had increased his lands, too, at the foot of Mt. Diablo. He had dreams of selling the land to other Americans and had pamphlets printed which he sent back to the states, describing the new country. He urged people to come and told them he would sell them land cheaply. He had got some of his land from dishonest Mexican officials for very little. The old settlers and their sons heard about these pamphlets that were being sent about their land, and they were worried. They realized that some of their own government officials were not honest men and were taking bribes from the greedy aliens for land. In the meetings in Jacob Leese's store, someone said that there was very little money left in the treasury. The men of Yerba Buena wondered what should be done. When they heard that *Comandante* Vallejo had moved his whole family to the presidio at Sonoma, everyone was afraid. There were only a dozen ragged soldiers left at the presidio to guard the port. The people stayed in their adobe houses and no longer were pleased to see new faces arriving from the ships in the bay.

They thought perhaps things would be better when Governor Alvarado ordered the outlaw, Isaac Graham, to leave California. But there were other bad men who stole and who sold grog to Indians and created disturbances in the village. New people were coming over the mountains and through the portals to the Pacific Ocean. At last *Comandante* Vallejo wrote to the head of the government in Mexico and told of the troubles the colony was having.

It was not until 1842, though, that the Mexican government did anything for the colonists. Then Governor Alvarado was replaced by another

*The Mexican soldiers were a ragged band of robbers
and murderers who stole and killed as they pleased.*

governor. The new man, Manuel Micheltorena, was a courtly gentleman just as Governor Alvarado had been. Mexico sent at the same time a small army of soldiers. They were men who had been released from prison camps to come to the new land. They were a ragged band of murderers and robbers, and their conduct was even worse than that of the foreigners. They stole from the people and killed anyone they chose. The people of California complained because Mexico had sent such a band to their country, but the new governor didn't seem able to help.

Again Mexico replaced the governor, this time with a man named Pio Pico. Pio Pico tried his best to get the gringos, or foreigners, to leave the country and to stop stealing the land and cattle. By now there were too many people who were not Mexican subjects in California. These people began to feel that the land really belonged to them and they wouldn't leave.

8 THE NEW VILLAGE

The people of Yerba Buena, like others in California, felt that they were forsaken by Mexico. It took so long for word to get back and forth and, when orders did come, the Californians didn't like what Mexico told them to do. It seemed to them that Mexico had lost all interest in the colony on San Francisco Bay. The people feared that soon another country would take possession of their land.

The ships of England and Russia and many from the United States were in and out of the harbor all of the time.

Many Americans had come by this time, some with their families. San Franciscans heard the Americans say that California really should be a state in their union. The Spaniards liked the Americans because they were a friendly people. They liked them better than they did the Russians and the English, but still they didn't like the idea of any country taking over their land. Some of the Spanish officials heard that the United States had offered to buy California and that Mexico had refused.

A few years after Sutter settled on the banks of the Sacramento River, a young army officer, John C. Frémont, came riding into California with a band of trappers. He had been sent by the United States government to explore the western country. He was asked to follow the trails and make maps for the government. It was the same sort of expedition that Anza had made for Spain seventy years before.

These men came over the rugged Sierra Nevada, the "Snowy Range," in mid-winter, but managed to get through the high passes on snowshoes. The famous guide and trapper, Kit Carson, was one of

A band of trappers made their way to California over the snowy passes of the rugged Sierra Nevada.

the party, and a high pass in the mountains is still called Kit Carson Pass. At Sutter's Fort the men rested, and Sutter gave them fresh horses on which to continue their journey. The men rode on down through the valleys, beautiful with flowers now for it was springtime. Frémont wrote home that he never had seen such a beautiful land. They rode over the Tehachapi Mountains, over Tejon Pass, through the Mojave Desert, and followed the old Spanish trail out of the state.

Frémont wrote a complete report of his travels, and when the government printed thousands of copies there was great excitement among the Americans. People by the hundred wanted to go to the new land. Wagon trains started across the plains every day with whole families to settle in a land where there was plenty of food and where the climate was mild all of the year.

There was nothing now that the Spanish people could do to stop the Americans from coming. There were too many of them, and most of the men came armed. In the army posts there were pitifully few Spanish soldiers.

These new people were filled with energy. They settled in the wide valleys, cut down trees and built wooden houses. They farmed the land themselves and didn't depend on servants to do their work for them as the Spaniards had done.

During this time the United States was fighting with Mexico over Texas. It seemed very far away to the Californians. They were used to hearing that their country was fighting with someone. They weren't very excited about it, but their new American neighbors could talk of nothing else.

Finally one day, the bold Captain Frémont arrived in California again. He came with a group of hardy men dressed in deerskin and carrying guns. The Californians became restless once more. They liked the American farmers, but Americans riding horses and carrying guns were a different matter. Besides, the Californians had heard that the President of the United States, James K. Polk, wanted very much to have a good harbor on the West Coast. And hadn't this same young explorer, John C. Frémont, made all kinds of maps of their country and given them to the people of his country? And hadn't the gringos been able to follow the maps all the way across the plains and the mountains to California? The officials and the older men shook their heads and sighed. It was all a bad business, but they had no idea what they could do.

Their own country had her troubles nearer at home. So the Californians greeted the newcomers politely and offered them hospitality as they had always done and said nothing. But their eyes were dark with fear, and they were sad and felt forgotten by everyone.

The young Captain again told the Californians that he was only on a surveying trip, but they didn't believe him. Some of his band boasted that if they were attacked by California soldiers they would fight to kill. The Californians recognized this as a threat because everyone knew that no California soldier ever attacked anyone. They felt that the end of Mexican rule was very near and that soon their land would be part of the United States.

In June, 1846, Frémont and his band decided to march to Sonoma and call on the *comandante*, Don Mariano Vallejo. Don Mariano was most courteous to his rough visitors and invited them into the house for food and drink in the true California manner. He realized with great sorrow that the end of Mexican rule was near. Quietly he discussed terms with the Americans.

After this bold visit to the commander, the Americans didn't know whether their country would want them to raise the American flag or not. So they talked together for a little while and then said, "We have decided to make California a free republic, not Mexican and not American." One of

Frémont came with a group of hardy men carrying guns.

the Americans took a large piece of cloth and painted a big red star in one corner. He painted a large brown bear in the center. Then from a red flannel shirt he tore a strip and sewed it along the bottom of the canvas. Above the strip were printed the words "California Republic."

The flag was raised over the plaza in Sonoma. As they watched the flag hoisted in the summer breeze, the villagers whispered to one another that the bear looked like a greedy Yankee pig with a long snout.

The Americans repaid Vallejo's hospitality by sending him and his brother-in-law, Jacob Leese, up the river to Sutter's fort as prisoners of war.

Now that the Bear Flag floated over the plaza, Frémont and his men didn't know what to do next. They roamed up and down the countryside, picking fights with Mexican soldiers, while the women and children stayed in their houses in terror.

Soon afterward, though, word came that Mexico was actually at war with the United States. When Frémont's men heard that, they quickly pulled down the Bear Flag and raised the flag of the United States. Frémont was a member of the army, and now he was ready to fight for his country. American ships came into the harbors of Monterey and San Francisco. There wasn't very much fighting, but now that the Californians were really at war they fought bravely. The war ended in the southern part of the state when Andres Pico gave up and surrendered to Frémont at Cahuenga Pass.

During this short war the little village of Yerba Buena hardly knew what was going on in the rest of California. One day the villagers came out of their adobes to see the American ship *Portsmouth* come sailing into the harbor flying the Stars and Stripes. Then a British ship came flying the Union Jack. The people wondered, as they watched the ships of the two countries, if there would be a sea battle before their eyes. They thought it would be interesting to watch.

There was just a single shot from the American ship, and the British ship didn't return it. The people lost interest and went indoors to their siestas. Soon they were awakened by the roll of drums and the sound of marching feet. When they came out of their houses to see what was happening, they saw Captain Montgomery of the *Portsmouth* marching at the head of seventy marines and sailors toward the plaza. Soon the Stars and Stripes fluttered from the customs house. This time the guns from the *Portsmouth* boomed twenty-one times out in the bay, and all the Americans cheered.

The people of Yerba Buena now saw that this was the end of the California that they knew. The energetic Americans had taken over.

The Americans named the old plaza Portsmouth Square, and the long street along the water front they called Montgomery after the captain of the *Portsmouth*. A new alcalde was elected for Yerba Buena. He was an American, a lieutenant from the *Portsmouth*. His name was Washington A. Bartlett. Alcalde Bartlett appointed a man named O'Farrell to survey the village again. This he did, naming the streets for Americans. Those streets have the same names today—Montgomery, Kearny, O'Farrell, Mason, Powell and Stockton.

Events had never happened so fast in the village before. In less than a month a ship came sailing into the bay from the Hawaiian Islands with a group of 150 Mormons on board. They started out with the idea of forming a religious colony on the shores of San Francisco Bay. The men of the party all carried rifles, and the people in the village were uneasy once more. When the Mormons saw that there were so many Americans in the village, they thought twice before using their rifles. The women and children of the party were taken into homes, and the men put up wooden shacks and set up tents on the hills for the men of the party.

The people of the village marveled at all the things the Mormon settlers brought with them. They had real mattresses stuffed with moss, and bed sheets of linen and calico, pots and pans and dishes, mechanic's tools, even a printing press. The California women were puzzled by the wives of the Mormons who rushed about the village in unbecoming wrappers of gray and blue calico, with their hair pulled tightly into a little knot. The Mormon women hardly smiled at all but hurried from errand to errand with grim, determined faces.

The beautiful Spanish ladies, with their rippling silk gowns and lace mantillas, thought it unwise for the ladies not to pay more attention to their dress.

As they went about making over the Spanish village into an American town, the new people treated the old residents of Yerba Buena as if they didn't exist. Sam Brannan, the Mormon leader, established the first newspaper the village ever had in January, 1847. He called it *The California Star*.

It was in this newspaper that the announcement was made that the name of the village was no longer Yerba Buena. Alcalde Bartlett proclaimed the change to San Francisco.

Gradually, with more and more Americans coming on every ship, the small village of San Francisco was more American than Spanish. At the end of May, 1847, when news came that General Taylor had won a victory over the Mexicans at Buena Vista, there was great rejoicing among the Americans and among the old San Franciscans as well. The American flag flew over every old adobe and all the new wooden houses as well as over the flimsy tents where the workingmen lived on the steep hills. Bonfires crackled on the sand dunes, and fireworks were shot off for days. There was dancing in Portsmouth Square with everybody joining in the festivities.

The town of San Francisco, with its mixture of many kinds of people from all over the world, was prospering. Wharves had been built along the water front to take care of the shiploads of goods that came into the port from all over the world.

The new government worked well, and there was law and order among the people. Young men who had come alone to the port were marrying into the old families and building homes for themselves on the steep hills. There was plenty for everyone, and life was gay. The people were happy and content once more. Soon all this was to change.

9 GOLD AND THE NEW STATE

The rumor of gold in the hills was no new thing to the old settlers of California. In the early days, Indians had brought gold to the mission fathers and had gladly exchanged it for a few glass beads or a little tobacco.

In March of 1848, the people of San Francisco heard that gold had been discovered in a mill-race belonging to John Augustus Sutter by a carpenter who worked for him, James Marshall. But they didn't pay any attention to the rumor. Some men said it was just a tall tale made up by Sutter to get people to buy land from him. People remembered that two years before Sutter had allowed his fort to be turned into a prison for the good *comandante* Vallejo and the storekeeper Jacob Leese. They remembered, too, how he had sold furs to the Russians at Fort Ross before they left the country in 1841.

Even the Americans said that this rumor was just a scheme of Sutter's to get people to the hills so he could sell them supplies from his stores. So men in San Francisco went about their affairs and forgot the rumor.

But soon people began to miss familiar faces in the village. The tables at the boarding houses were nearly empty. Someone said that John Marsh was not at his *rancho* in the shadow of Mt. Diablo and that his Indian servants wouldn't tell where he had gone. Sam Brannan couldn't be found at home or in any of the business houses of the town.

Then one day Sam Brannan appeared again. His beard was ragged and dirty, and his eyes were wild with excitement. Up and down the streets of San Francisco he ran holding a bottle of gold dust high above his head, and shouting at the top of

Brannan ran up and down the street shouting, "Gold!"

his lungs, "Gold! Gold! Gold from the American River!"

The whole of San Francisco went mad with excitement. Men left by boat across the bay and up the rivers toward the hills. Some left by mule and horseback, and others started walking. Even the slow-moving Spaniards wrapped their serapes about them, mounted their horses and galloped off toward the gold a hundred miles from San Francisco. The inns, the grog shops and places of business were deserted. The little church on the plaza held no services. All the men rushed away, afraid the gold would be gone before they could get their share. Only the women and children were left in the village. Soldiers deserted their posts and took the army horses as well as supplies. Blankets, guns and knives that belonged to the presidio went with them. Other soldiers were sent after the deserters; but, when they got to the hills, they joined the others and stayed to dig for the precious gold.

Many ships tossed idly in the bay without a man aboard. The crews had gone to find their share of the treasure, too. Finally the alcalde padlocked the door of his office and followed the others.

Sutter, the man who had dreamed of having his own kingdom in the new land, had so far been quite successful. He had thousands of cattle, mules and horses on his many acres. Hundreds of Indians worked for him for very little money. He was one of the most powerful men in the new land. However, from the moment gold was discovered on his land, his power was gone. His men deserted in hundreds to go to the gold fields. Indians, white men and Kanakas ran off to the hills. When they left, they stole from his trading post everything they could carry. They even took the grinding stones from his new flour mill. They took the bells from the tower in the fort and the cannon he had brought with him from Switzerland. People drove off his horses and cattle at night. The man with so many dreams of wealth had nothing left.

After the first excitement of the discovery of gold was over, many of the men who had gone from San Francisco came back to their homes. Digging gold was hard work, and men who had lived in town were not used to bending their backs and using a pick on the hard ground. They knew, too, that the miners would need supplies. So the men who had shops in San Francisco came back and let the other men stay to dig in the hills.

San Francisco had its share of the excitement just the same. The city grew to three times its size in a few weeks. It took a few months for the word of gold to get to the East Coast and to the rest of the world. But when it did, the bay began to fill with ships and barges. Many Americans came the long way around Cape Horn by ship, and others took the dangerous journey across the Isthmus of Panama and then by boat up the West Coast. One vessel, the *S.S. California*, arrived from Panama with four hundred men, all of them sick with jungle fever. They were packed so closely on the little ship that they couldn't walk on deck.

Many people tried the hard trip over the mountains by oxcart and prairie schooner. A great many of these men and women and children died of cold and hunger and disease. Some of them were killed by Indians along the way.

Not only Americans came to seek gold. Ships sailed across the Pacific Ocean into the bay of San Francisco, bringing hundreds of Chinese and men from the continent of Australia. All were headed for the fields of gold they had heard about. There were men, too, from Chile and Peru in South America. There were rich men and poor men and thieves and convicts from all over the world arriving in the port every week. As soon as they arrived, they quickly bought a pick and shovel and blankets and food in San Francisco and started out for the hills.

Some of the wiser men just stayed in the hills

for a short time and then returned to San Francisco to set up in business. They knew that they would get the gold by selling needed supplies to the miners for high prices, and it wouldn't be such hard work.

Soon the hills and the sand lots of San Francisco were covered with wooden shacks. The main part of the town around the plaza was jammed with stores and gambling halls and boarding houses.

Now the old Californians were greatly outnumbered by the newcomers. They still tried to live their lives in their own way. They had their usual fiestas and fandangos and picnics in the country, but the Americans were really running the city.

When all the foreigners hastily ran off to the hills with their picks and shovels, one old Spanish don, Luis Peralta, who had lived a hundred years, advised his sons: "My sons, God has given this gold to the Americans. If He had wanted us to have it, He would have given it to us before this. So I tell you, do not go after it. Plant your lands and gather your crops. These are your best gold fields."

As it turned out, Don Luis Peralta had given his sons wise advice. After the great flurry of the gold rush was over in later years, the people of California found that their rich farm lands were

From the lookout point he saw the flag had a new star.

much more valuable than the gold from the mountains.

In January, 1848, when James Marshall found the first flakes of gold and reported it to Sutter, California was still under an American military governor, and all of the old-time Spanish Californians still obeyed their own laws and still had their own alcaldes. The military governor and his army simply watched over things and waited patiently for Congress in Washington to do something about the new territory. Congress had troubles close at home, though, and California seemed very far away.

But after the real gold rush was under way and hordes of Americans flocked into California, these new Californians wanted their own laws and their own system of government. They wanted California to be one of the United States.

First, though, the new territory had to have a constitution of its own. So a group of men, without waiting for Congress to act, called a meeting of lawmakers in Monterey. They drew up a code of laws, levied taxes and elected Peter H. Burnett as their first governor.

Not until September 9, 1850, did Congress pass a bill admitting California to the Union. But still the people in California didn't know that they were a state, and they waited patiently for news. A man was stationed each day in the lookout station on top of Telegraph Hill in San Francisco to watch for ships coming in through the Golden Gate.

One day in late October, the man in the station saw a ship sailing through the Golden Gate with many American flags flying. When he saw a very large flag fluttering from the mast, where he could count thirty-one stars, he knew that at last California was a state.

He rushed down the steep hill shrieking the news to everyone, "California is the thirty-first state." People came from all over and scrambled up the hill to look for themselves. The American ship *Oregon* came steadily on into the harbor as the people cheered from the hilltop.

When the ship docked, Californians found out that they had been a state of the Union for six weeks and hadn't known it.

There was a great celebration in San Francisco. Riders were quickly sent to San Jose, the capital, to tell the news. They spread the word to everyone along the way, too. For days the celebration went on with fireworks and parades and speeches in all the mining camps and towns in the new state.

A flag with a bright new star fluttered over the plaza in the American city of San Francisco for the first time.

10 LAW ENFORCEMENT AND VIGILANTES

In most cities the laws of the community are made as they are needed. But when a small, peaceful village of just two hundred people grows in a few short years to a city of thousands, the laws of the village can't meet the laws for so many more people. The first settlers, too, were mostly law-abiding in Yerba Buena, but when the city of San Francisco emerged, the people were quite different. There were good men and women still; but there were

"The Hounds" hung around the wharves stealing cargo.

evil men, a great many of them, who came to the raw new city to seek their fortunes.

First of all, there was sent from New York a group of soldiers in 1847 to join Captain Frémont in the small war. But they didn't arrive in time to do any fighting. Then, when the rush came to the gold fields, they were too late to stake out any claims for gold. Angrily they came back to San Francisco and spent most of their time hanging around the wharves on the water front, stealing cargo and bullying the people who were not American. These and others were "The Hounds." They found ready companions to join them in a group of Australians, convicts who had been shipped out of their own country to California. These Australians were widely known as "Sydney Ducks." These two groups of bullies had fine sport in looting stores and ships, and frightening innocent people. Finally they began to carry rifles and one Hound assaulted a Spanish-Californian. The Californian fought back and accidentally killed a bystander. This is just what the Hounds had hoped for. Now they could say that the Spaniards were dangerous people and should be driven out of the city. The Hounds all cried out against the Spaniards and the Chinese, the Indians and the people from South America. They said they all should go. These evil men now changed their name to "The Regulators" and began to go about the town acting as if they were the officers of the law. At the foot of Telegraph Hill one Sunday morning, they shot their rifles into the air and so badly terrorized the wives of the Chileans who lived there that word was sent to the alcalde. The alcalde was almost helpless to deal with these people because his police force hadn't grown along with the town. Something had to be done quickly.

Sam Brannan, the Mormon Elder who had run through the village shouting "Gold," was now one of the older citizens. He decided to stop these ruffians and called a meeting of good citizens in Portsmouth Square. These men suspected, too, that the Sydney Ducks had been setting fires on the water front, but they had no proof. There had been a frightful fire on Christmas Eve in 1849 that had destroyed half the town.

So Sam Brannan managed to get 230 men together to act as a police force. They chose a brave man named William Spofford for their leader. In a very short time twenty Hounds were caught and put in the brig aboard the *U.S.S. Warren*. Their trial was speedy, and in no time at all the leaders were convicted and sent out of the country.

The rest of the criminals hid out, and the good people of the town went about their business. But still there were fires. The police knew that they were set deliberately, but they were unable to find the culprits.

The volunteer police force went about their own affairs. The few city officials were too busy counting their gold to pay attention to the city government. The courts were very lax, and the judges were not competent. Most important, there were too few police.

The bad men took advantage of this, and there was another wave of crime in the city. Miners, down from the hills with canvas pouches filled with gold dust, were easy victims. Each day some of them were found dead or unconscious along the muddy streets and the water fronts, with their gold dust gone. In the early part of 1851 two thugs entered the shop of a man named Jansen, knocked him over the head and made off with his money. This wasn't really as bad as some of the things that had been going on, but it was enough to set the people off. The newspaper *Alta California* ran an indignant article about the outrage and asked how long the citizens were going to stand such things.

The police did catch two men who were identified by the dying Jansen as the ones who had cracked his skull. The men were nearly hanged by the angry mob; but cooler judgment, after finding only the evidence of a sick man, released the men.

This time Sam Brannan and other citizens persuaded a good man of the community, William T. Coleman, to organize and head a vigilance committee. Sam Brannan gave a room in his store for the meetings of the committee. The committee members were mostly volunteer firemen. They agreed on a signal which was to be two taps on the fire-engine bell to call them to duty.

The very next day the two taps on the bell rang out. A thief named Jenkins was caught stealing an iron safe from the water front. The thief thought he would get off with the easy-going officials of the court, but he didn't know how stern the new Vigilance Committee could be. The committee didn't even take him to court, but gave him a speedy trial in their committee room, while the angry crowd waited. Finally Mr. Brannan stepped outside and told the crowd that they had decided to hang Jenkins, but that everything was to be done properly. He told them even a minister had been sent for. The thief was hanged that night from the old adobe in the public square. This was the first hanging to take place in San Francisco.

The crime wave abated for a while. The Vigilance Committee continued to have trials and settle questions without interference. On the whole they were fair and honest in their decisions, and the people were so busy with other things that they let the committee do their work for them.

By the end of 1851 the work of this first Vigilance Committee was over. During the year they had banished from the city over thirty bad men, and their dealing out of quick justice frightened away many more. They had hanged four men from the gallows in all.

There were other public-spirited citizens of the town who didn't agree that the manner in which the self-appointed Vigilance Committee worked was the right way. They knew that it wasn't the lawful way. So they organized another party and called themselves the Law and Order Party. Their plan was to help the regular officials of the town who had been duly appointed to office or elected by law.

During the years between 1852 and 1856 we hear no more of the famous Vigilance Committee. Huge fires continued to break out on the water front, burning valuable cargo. Some of the fires—there were six large ones in five years—were blamed on the Sydney Ducks, many of whom still lived under the wharves and in the crowded inns for sailors.

The *Alta California* ran articles telling the people that the town needed cleaning out again. They said that the bad men must go. They suggested that the Vigilance Committee meet again.

Meanwhile a new kind of vice was in the city. This time it was dishonest politics. Politicians were stuffing ballot boxes at election time. Honest voters were afraid to go to the polls to vote for fear they would be shouldered away by a bunch of bullies. Political conventions were a farce, and none of the best citizens took any interest in city government. They let the incompetent men get into office and run the city to suit themselves. In one year a thousand men were killed in the city, and only one by process of law.

At last *The Bulletin*, a newspaper edited by an honest young man called James King of William, began printing editorials protesting the corrupt methods of the officials. He exposed the bad men and named them in his paper. The good citizens of San Francisco were behind him and cheered him on in his exposures.

Then in one issue of his paper in May, 1856, King named and denounced James Casey, a ballot-stuffing politician. Casey blustered his way into King's office, and the editor coldly ordered him out.

Casey waited that evening until King left his office, and in full view of several passers-by Casey shot the editor. Quickly his crooked friends surrounded him and bore him off to jail where they were sure he would be quite safe, as he had so many friends in high places. For six days the young editor lingered between life and death, and his friends waited anxiously. The whole city was in a terrific state of excitement. Finally it was announced that King was dead, and the feeling in the city was high. The pistol shot that had killed the editor sent off the greatest feeling of mob violence so far.

Soon a crowd gathered outside the prison and loudly and angrily demanded that Casey be brought out. The jailers secretly took him to the county jail on Dupont Street, but there they found another mob waiting and shrieking in a frenzy for their victim. Some of the mob whispered that the Vigilance Committee was meeting once more, and that cooled down the angry mob of ten thousand men for the night so nothing happened.

A guard of well-armed men was left to watch the prisoner. Meanwhile the Vigilance Committee was meeting. Coleman took the oath of office, and the books were open for enrollment. It was resolved that the Committee should go at once to the jail and demand Casey and another murderer called Cora, and give them a trial and just punishment. The sheriff let the Committee take his prisoners. His men were so vastly outnumbered by the mob that there was nothing else he could do.

While the mile-long funeral procession of James King of William was slowly moving through the streets, the bodies of Casey and Cora were swinging from wooden beams in front of the Vigilance Committee quarters.

By July of 1856 the Committee had six thousand men under arms, all well equipped and organized into different groups, like an army with officers to command them. The building where they met they called Fort Vigilance. It was really a fort, too. There were cannons placed on the corners of the roof and sentinels stationed on the roof as well. Around the building the men erected a high wall of gunny sacks stuffed with sand, and in each corner of this wall was a cannon. The fort was nicknamed *Fort Gunnybags* by the people of San Francisco.

The Vigilance Committee became so powerful that criminals from distant towns all over California were brought to San Francisco for trial before the Committee. They gave decisions on crimes that were committed at sea, personal disagreements, and fraud in money matters. In fact the Committee would decide any kind of disagreement, no matter how small, if the persons came before them.

The Vigilantes were now so powerful that some of their bolder members even suggested that it was time to proclaim the new state an independent Pacific Republic with the men of vigilance in control.

Finally the Governor of the state realized that the Committee was getting too powerful and asked General Sherman to take charge of the state

militia, in a protest move against the Vigilantes.
General Sherman asked General Wool of the Ben-
icia Arsenal for arms and permission to go to San
Francisco and take a stand against the Vigilantes.
When the Committee in San Francisco heard of
the plan of the militia, they added reinforcements
to their barricade and were prepared to fight the
authorities. They ordered a bigger bell to call
their members to arms and waited. Meanwhile
General Sherman consulted with General Wool.
At first General Wool promised to give the neces-
sary guns, and then thought better of it and with-
drew his permission. General Sherman was bitterly
disappointed. His plan, so he said, was just to go to
San Francisco with a show of arms. He was sure
the unlawful band would break up when they saw
the armed forces of the United States.

Perhaps General Wool was wise. There might
have been dreadful fighting in the streets of San
Francisco if General Sherman had challenged the
Vigilantes. At this time they were at the height of
their power and very cocksure. Wiser men in the
city felt that despite the good work the Vigilantes
were doing it wasn't a safe thing for so many men
to have so much power not under the law. If General Wool had allowed General Sherman to take
an army to the city with rifles to oppose the Vig-

ilantes, who also had all the guns and ammunition they needed, it might have ended in a great disaster.

At last in the summer, the Vigilantes announced that their work was no longer needed and they decided to disband. The majority of the citizens of the city were greatly relieved. Now the American people in the new frontier city would govern themselves under the laws of the state and the nation.

11   SHOWERS OF SILVER

In the late 1850's, gold still was being mined in great quantities in the hills of California, and it poured into San Francisco. Then in 1859 silver was discovered in the Nevada hills. The famous Comstock Lode produced the precious metal in large amounts and this, too, flowed into San Francisco. The young city was rich beyond the wildest dreams of anyone. The great silver kings of Nevada came to San Francisco to build their mansions atop the hills that overlooked the bay. Fortunes were won and lost in a day. The little village that Colonel Anza had founded nearly a hundred years before was a thriving metropolis and no longer dependent upon the scanty supplies brought by ship from Mexico. Every citizen dreamed of acquiring great wealth from the gold and silver and the fruitful land.

Great distances had been conquered, too. The slow covered wagons still toiled across the plains, but now steamboats connected with the overland route across the Isthmus of Panama. John Butterfield's Stage Line ran regularly between St. Louis, Missouri, and San Francisco. By the end of 1858 it covered that great distance in twenty-one days.

In 1859 the Pony Express was making the hazardous journey across the mountains and plains to carry the mail. President Lincoln's message to Congress reached San Francisco in seven days and seventeen hours.

During the sad time just before the Civil War, there were a great many Southerners in San Francisco. Feeling again ran high in the city between the group who were for the Union and those who believed in the Southern Confederacy. Because of the great amount of gold and silver that was constantly flowing through the city, many of the Southerners tried their best to swing the people toward the South. The South needed money to carry on the war. Many of the federal employees were Southerners. The military commander was a Secessionist from Kentucky. Many of the ministers were from the South and on Sundays would pray openly for victory for the Confederacy. The situation became quite dangerous, and feeling ran high between the two factions.

Thomas Starr King, a spirited young Unitarian minister from Boston, was actually the one who saved San Francisco and the whole state for the Union by his fiery oratory. His contribution was so great that he is honored in Statuary Hall in Washington along with other great men.

His sermons from the pulpit were so fiery against slavery that some of the leading rebels were hanged in effigy in the city. He didn't hesitate to tell the people what their duty was to their country. Finally the Southern army officer, Albert Sidney Johnston, was relieved of his command and went home to Kentucky to join the Confederate Army. There were many plots among the loyal Southerners, but all these failed and the men who hatched them left the city by government invitation.

After the Civil War, the population of San Francisco had grown to nearly 100,000. This was an era of great prosperity and its people were, for the most part, reckless and young. The older Spaniards had moved to their *ranchos* or else stayed in retirement and were seldom seen. The new people had taken over the growing city. People from all over the world had migrated to the last frontier port.

Adventurous Americans were in the majority, but there were Chinese who settled in one section of the city with their own customs and specch. The French formed another colony and the Mexicans, new Mexicans from northern Mexico, stayed pretty much to themselves in another group.

Many Italians, some of them coming as early as 1840, settled in North Beach where the bay reminded them of their own seas at home. The old wharf, Meiggs Wharf, was called Fisherman's Wharf, and the fishing industry which the town hadn't had time to think about with all the rush of growing, began with the Italian fishermen. They would sail out through the rough waters of the Golden Gate at dawn in their sturdy boats fluttering with painted sails, and they would come in by late afternoon, the boats laden with the large Pacific crabs and the tiny shrimp, sole, bass and sea trout. They sold their fish from the wharf, boiling the live crabs in huge caldrons, or peddled it from door to door. Fishing by the middle 1860's had become an important industry.

Chinatown, adjoining North Beach, was a crowded section. The flimsy houses had pagoda roofs and window frames brightly painted in red, blue, orange and yellow. Shaky balconies were crowded with porcelain bowls, sprouting with narcissi; and paper lanterns in red, yellow and blue danced on wires strung across the narrow main street.

In food shops whole pigs were strung up, smoked and baked to a rich brown; ducks, too, dry and as flat as if they had been pressed between the pages of an enormous book. The men wore blue padded jackets and wound their braided hair in a neat bun on the back of their heads. The women hobbled painfully up and down the steep hills on tiny feet that had been bound tightly when they were babies. They wore long black cotton trousers and tight jackets over them, buttoned high about their throats. Sometimes a flash of jade would sparkle in their night-black hair.

With its many different people in their native dress, the city in the sixties looked more European than American. On top of Nob Hill, the palaces

The Chinese crowded into their own section of town.

of the rich men looked down on Chinatown and North Beach in a lordly manner.

The town had an American flavor, too. In the sixties there were over a dozen churches of different creeds. The city had an annual fair. There was a May fete each year where children from all the schools danced around the Maypole in Portsmouth Square. Most of the schoolteachers came from Boston, so young San Franciscans learned to talk with a New England accent.

The French and Italian immigrants established restaurants where the food was European in flavor and the prices were high. But there was plenty of money; and although people grumbled about it, they paid the high prices. The ladies of the community didn't have to wait for the fashion magazines to come the long route by boat from the East. They had their own fashion magazine, *The Hesperian*, that told them about the latest word in style from Paris and New York. It was illustrated, too, and looked very much like *Godey's Lady's Book*.

American ladies practiced elocution and gave dramatic readings from Shakespeare and Longfellow. There were the theater and the opera, where even the children attended evening performances. The city was enthusiastic about opera and San

Franciscans thought nothing of paying five dollars a seat to hear their favorites.

There were plenty of servants, mostly Chinese, since they were the only ones who worked for small wages in San Francisco. Gold and silver were still plentiful. Business houses had sprung up in solid blocks along the water front. Wells, Fargo carried letters and parcels and shipped large quantities of gold, silver and other valuables. Under the new laws, the loan companies organized into banks and became powerful companies. During the need for mining implements, due to the slow transportation from the East Coast, the city was compelled to manufacture the tools herself. The Union Iron Works, begun in 1849, had expanded so that by 1865 its implements were known around the world. By the end of the sixties San Francisco had over forty foundries and machine shops.

12 SAN FRANCISCO ANNEXES THE UNITED STATES

The first pilgrims coming with Anza from Mexico hadn't been in San Francisco long before they experienced an earthquake. The Indians laughed at their fears and told the Spaniards that it was the custom of the earth to shiver occasionally. It did no damage. So the men and women built up the mud walls of their houses that had fallen down.

When in a few months or a year the earth rumbled and shook again, they built their houses over once more and reminded each other that it made no difference. The shocks were never very violent and the people accepted them. There is no record of anyone being killed during those first seventy years, although during that period there were three or four shocks a year.

When the Americans came to the port, though, and began building houses of wood rather than adobe, the earthquakes became more alarming. In 1856, when the town was filled with shacks of flimsy wood, there was a violent shock. Several of the frame houses were completely overturned and brick chimneys fell, killing several people. Eleven years later, with mild shocks in the years between, there was another severe quake and many larger buildings were broken to pieces and flattened. Then in 1872 there was a violent temblor. Large public buildings had been built by this time, and their walls were split and cracked. The rumble and shaking of the earth caused quite a panic for the time, and there was some loss of life.

During these early times the quake was felt mostly on the shifting ground near the water front. A great deal of this ground was man-made, filled with sand dredged up from the bottom of the bay. Some families, feeling safer on the more solid hills, moved back from the water. But the business firms stayed where they were, rebuilding each time their buildings were damaged.

So the people became accustomed to the slight shocks, and were amused at the look of surprise and fright on a visitor's face when the earth trembled.

So many exciting events were taking place that they didn't have time to give much thought to earthquakes. Men didn't feel quite so remote from the rest of the country now that the telegraph was completed. The first message the city sent over the new wires that strung across the land was to President Lincoln. The message said the people of San Francisco hoped that there would always be "a bond of perpetuity between the states of the Atlantic and those of the Pacific."

With the coming of the telegraph, the Pony Express was finished. People began then to talk about a railroad across the whole country, from ocean to ocean. The young city was impatient with the slow transportation by boat around South America by steamer and sailing ship and the long overland route by stagecoach and mule team. The rancher wanted a quicker way of marketing his grain and his cattle, and the merchant wanted manufactured articles to arrive in weeks instead of months and at a cheaper rate of transportation. A railway would solve these problems.

A young engineer, Theodore D. Judah, had come to California in the early fifties to start building a railroad in the state. In two years he had built a railroad from Sacramento to the town of Folsom, a little over twenty miles distant. At this time Judah tried to interest influential men in laying a railroad across the high Sierras and across the Nevada desert and the plains beyond to meet the eastern rails that were by this time beyond the Mississippi. Many people, the shortsighted ones, laughed at the young engineer and called him a dreamer. But Judah wouldn't forget his dreams and persisted in his plans. It wasn't until July 1, 1862, that he succeeded in having Congress pass the Pacific Railroad Bill and President Lincoln signed it. Judah was in Washington at the time, and over the new telegraph wire sent the word to his friends in Sacramento who had helped him. He wired, "We have drawn the elephant, now let's see if we can hitch him up."

Judah didn't live to see his project completed.

The men left to carry out the task were Mark Hopkins, Charles Crocker, Collis P. Huntington and Leland Stanford. They were called "The Big Four."

The Union Pacific was to build westward over the route planned. The Central Pacific Company was to start at Sacramento and build east until the two lines joined, making a continuous railroad across the United States. From the beginning it was an exciting race between the two teams of workers to see which one would finish first.

The machinery for the Central Railroad had to be brought by sailing ship around Cape Horn, landed at San Francisco and taken from there to Sacramento by flat barges.

The Union Pacific transported its materials over local railways in Iowa and by Missouri River boats. The forests of the West were thick with fine hard timber for the heavy railroad ties, and lumber to build trestles across the rivers and the snowsheds along the mountain passes. The West had all this raw material, but the country was still wild and desolate. It took time to build the machine shops and the lumber mills before the work of actually laying the rails could even begin.

It was far easier for the Union Pacific to build

the tracks across the flat prairies where material and shops were closer at hand.

Both companies had to employ countless laborers to do the hard, back-breaking work. The Californians sent for thousands of Chinese, who would work for very little, to come from Canton. The Union Pacific hired thousands of Irish immigrants to dig the rail beds and lay the heavy rails. The Irish, too, worked for small wages. They had come to this country in large numbers because of the great potato famine in Ireland. After months of starvation and sickness across the ocean, they were glad of enough food to eat and a little money for clothes.

The work of the railroads, despite all the many hardships, progressed rapidly. The workers were eager to press on each day and get to new country. They listened eagerly to trappers and Indians who brought word of how far the other workers had come, and doubled their efforts. The bosses put on more men, too, so that the rails would flash across the deserts and the mountains as soon as possible. At one time, when both companies were racing at top speed to finish their section first, there were twenty-five thousand men working the long span across the country.

One day toward the end of the great race, Charles Crocker succeeded in having his Chinese workmen lay, in a single day, ten miles and one hundred and eighty feet of railroad track. Everyone in the whole country waited breathlessly for the rails to join. Finally on May 10, 1869, the word flashed over the new telegraph wires. The rails were joined at Promontory Point, Utah. Wherever there was a telegraph the people listened. It was arranged so that the first blows of the heavy sledge hammer driving in the final spike would be signaled over the wires.

At Promontory Point, where the formal ceremony was held, there was great rejoicing. Leaning on their picks and shovels, thousands of Chinese and Irish rested at last and watched the men who had planned the tremendous joining of East and West giving speeches, dressed in their cutaways and top hats. Indians on their wild ponies, dressed in their finest buffalo robes and gaudy feathers, gathered to watch the white man's magic.

They saw the men of Arizona present their spikes of silver, gold and iron, and the representatives of Nevada give the spike of silver. Then the men from California laid in place a polished tie of laurel and drove into it a shining golden spike with firm taps from a silver hammer. After the golden spike was driven into the hard wood, the Central Pacific train backed up and let the Union Pacific train and locomotive roll back and forth across the joined rails. Then the Central Pacific repeated the ceremony.

The great task was completed and the cheering started. Train whistles blasted shrilly; Indians gave their war whoops; the Irish workers danced quick jig steps and threw their hats in the air, while the Chinese smiled and nodded to one another at the antics of the Americans. Cheers were given, one after another, for the Atlantic and the Pacific, for the men who had made the railroad possible, and for the thousands who had dug the ground and laid the heavy rails. The telegraph tapped out this historic message to the waiting world: "The last spike is driven! The Pacific Railroad is completed! The junction point is 1,086 miles west of the Missouri and 690 miles east of Sacramento City."

In San Francisco the people were delirious with joy as they listened to the news over the telegraph. As each blow struck in far-off Utah, a corresponding blow rang out from the bell on the City Hall. The old cannon was fired off at Fort Point by the Golden Gate. Men screamed themselves hoarse

A golden spike was driven into the polished tie that completed the first transcontinental railroad.

with joy. For three days the people celebrated. Bands played; flags waved from every building; and there were speeches and parades each day and dancing at night. At night men marched up and down the streets carrying transparencies. These were poles with thin cloth boxes, with torches blazing at each corner. On the cloth in bold red letters were the words, "San Francisco Annexes the United States!"

13 THE MAN WHO BUILT SAN FRANCISCO

After the completion of the transcontinental rail-road, with a connecting link which ran from Sacramento to Oakland, across the bay from San Francisco, business and industry began a rapid development. Whole families were coming to the West over the new rail line, as well as people from other countries who made the trip by sea to San Francisco. The new land was vast and fruitful, and any number of large families were easily absorbed.

When the railway was completed, however, the great numbers of Chinese who had worked laying the ties and hammering the spikes and cutting the trees, didn't have any reason to stay in the wilderness or the small villages. So they came back to San Francisco. Their friends were there, and they all congregated in one section of the city in squalid tenements. They could live on very little and went out as servants among the white people, or, if they had enough savings, set up small businesses in the Chinese district. Some of them peddled vegetables and fish or went about from house to house mending chairs and doing odd jobs. There were thousands of them in San Francisco, and soon there were mutterings among some of the American workingmen that the Chinese worked for too little and took the jobs from the Americans.

There were anti-Chinese riots. In the Chinese quarter some police officers were killed by the Chinese when they tried to make arrests. In turn, many Chinese were killed by the mobs of whites, and the rest of Chinatown was so terrorized that people hid out for days. Finally the feeling died down, and the Chinese were able to go about their affairs once more. Demonstrations continued in a mild way, but the police were able to deal with them. Not until six years later did the feeling against the Chinese rise again.

Meanwhile new excitement was bubbling in San Francisco. New veins of silver had been found in the Comstock in Nevada, and San Francisco was in a fever of excitement once more. Men didn't rush off to the mines with pick and shovel the way they had done in the fifties. This time money was needed to dig deep tunnels, build stamp mills and sink shafts deep into the dry Nevada earth. Crafty speculators moved into San Francisco overnight. Everybody wanted to be in on the new bonanza in Nevada. Men and women bought stock in silver mines that they had never seen. Some of these mines didn't even exist, but were just names on paper. The Chinese, always great gamblers, invested the dollars they had earned when they built the railroad across the high mountains.

The most important name in San Francisco during this period was that of William Chapman Ralston. People called him a financial wizard. Ralston had been in California for several years. He first came as the captain of a cargo and passenger ship from Panama. The next time he came it was to head his shipping company's business on Sacramento Street. Finally, in 1864, he founded the

Bank of California, the bank that was to become the most important depository for the millions that came from the Nevada Comstock.

Billy Ralston, as almost everyone in the city fondly called him, was a stocky, friendly man, with humorous blue eyes and a fine, sandy beard and side whiskers. His bank controlled the steamship lines that ran from San Francisco to the coast of Oregon, and the fast Pacific Mail that ran between California and the Orient. The bank also controlled the river steamers that plied between San Francisco and Sacramento and Stockton. These were the steamers that brought the wheat, meat, fruit, oil and great casks of wine to the port for shipment. In his way Ralston had more power in the city than any of the millionaires of the Comstock or the railroad builders. His bank did the business that controlled the economy of the city, and Ralston was a happy, busy man doing everything he could to make San Francisco the most fabulous port in the whole world.

The brokerage houses in the city at this time were running full blast. Everybody wanted to buy stocks in the new silver mines in Nevada. Men and women jostled one another in the queues to give their money to the brokers for stock certificates. Sometimes the crowds were so thick that the horsecars couldn't make their way over the narrow streets, and the whole city was in a turmoil.

Meanwhile the millions from Nevada were piling up in the vaults of the Bank of California and the other banks of the city. Ralston knew that there were 14,000,000 dollars in gold coin in the U. S. Sub-Treasury and he wanted to exchange his bullion for the gold coins as the coin in the bank was getting low. He knew that this was a right and proper transaction, but first he had to get permission from the Federal Government to make the exchange.

He wired President U. S. Grant in Washington and told the President there would be a panic if the banks ran out of coin and he couldn't make the exchange, but he got no reply. One morning Ralston opened the door of his bank and found that he had only fifty thousand dollars left in coin.

He knew that such a small amount could be drawn out by depositors in one day and the bank would have to close its doors. That decided him. He would prevent this on his own, since the President of the United States ignored his pleas.

Two of his loyal friends, Harpending and Doré, agreed to help him. At midnight the two met and walked together through the dimly lit streets to the bank. They wondered what their friend Ralston was up to. When they arrived at Ralston's office at the bank, they found him in high spirits. He cautioned them not to speak to anyone of what was about to take place. When Harpending asked him why the streets were so deserted, Ralston smiled and put his finger to his lips.

The three men walked silently through the deserted streets to the door of the United States Sub-Treasury. To his friends' amazement, the heavy bronze door swung open and Ralston disappeared inside. After a bit the door swung open, and Ralston came out dragging several heavy canvas sacks.

"Take these to the bank," he ordered his puzzled friends. "The gentleman there will give you something to bring back."

The two men hoisted the heavy sacks to their backs and did what Ralston told them to do.

At the Bank of California a trusted official took the sacks from them and in return gave them as many bars of Comstock silver as they could carry. Back at the Sub-Treasury they found Mr. Ralston waiting for them with more heavy sacks. They gave him the bars in exchange, and no one said a word.

All night long the men trudged wearily back and forth, exchanging the silver bars for gold coin.

No one interrupted them, no thugs attacked them, and no police were anywhere to be seen. Surely these friends of Ralston knew now, if they hadn't before, that Ralston was an all-powerful man in San Francisco.

The next morning anxious crowds milled around the doors of the bank. Whispers had been heard that there was no more coin in the vaults, and the people wanted their money or what there was left of it. The bank run was on.

The bank tellers at the windows looked worried as they saw the lines forming, and they didn't open the grilles at their windows.

"Why are you making so many of our customers wait?" Ralston asked in pretended surprise. "And on such a busy day? Come! Open up. Put more tellers on the windows and have your coin in hand."

More tellers appeared from nowhere. Trays laden with gold coin were rushed from the vaults and put at each teller's window. The people saw the shining coins, and they were relieved. The good news spread as quickly as the bad news had spread. Ralston had saved the Bank of California and had prevented a financial panic in the city.

If Ralston was worried about what President Grant would do to him for exchanging the silver bars for gold coin, he didn't show it. And then, after three days, word came from the President allowing gold to be exchanged for cash, so all was well. After Ralston saved the bank and the city from disaster, he had more friends than ever. His office at the bank was like the waiting room in a station. Women came to him for investment advice and for donations for their favorite charities. Men in business wanted his good will and wise judgment on their enterprises. He was an uncrowned king and his subjects loved him.

The theater was Mr. Ralston's special pet. Not only Mr. Ralston but the whole city loved to go to performances of any kind. Even the first settlers had their cockfights and bear and bull fights in the sandy arenas.

As soon as California became a state, San Francisco became a theater and opera city. Actors, usually adventurous, wanted to come to the frontier town even if it did mean a long, hard trip across the country or over the fever-infested jungles of Panama.

Most of the men who came to California were in their early twenties and thirties, so they loved entertainment of any kind. In the early 1850's, actors of national fame came to play Shakespeare in makeshift theaters by the light of whale-oil lamps and candles. If a performance pleased the audience, the actors were showered with coins and gold nuggets. Again, if actors after their long journey became ill, collections were promptly taken up among the townspeople and everyone rushed to their aid.

Edwin Booth, the famous Shakespearian actor, played in San Francisco often. In the early 1850's he played *Romeo and Juliet* to a cheering audience and showers of gold and silver coins. Lola Montez, famous then for her "Spider Dance," came to San Francisco many times. Everyone loved her dance and couldn't see it often enough. She concealed about her person corks in the shapes of spiders. These spiders were attached to almost invisible strings so that when the lovely Lola did her whirling dance, it looked as if spiders were all around her dancing in the air.

Lotta Crabtree was another theatrical favorite. Lotta came to the West as a young girl, properly chaperoned by her mother. She performed in the mining camps as well as in San Francisco. After playing in the West for many years, Lotta gave her farewell performance. She was still the idol of the city and the people hated to see her go. To show their appreciation on this last occasion they gave her a wreath of gold and a large package of twenty-dollar gold pieces.

Lotta later presented the city with a beautiful fountain with four carved lions' heads that still stands in the center of the city. Lotta's Fountain, it is called, and is the spot that the opera singer, Luisa Tetrazzini, chose to sing from when she gave her farewell to San Francisco many years later on a clear Christmas Eve.

With few exceptions the theaters themselves weren't very luxurious until the seventies. Any shelter was good enough to give a performance for the enthusiastic young audiences.

The first luxurious theater to be built was the Metropolitan in the year 1853, and it had its first performance on Christmas Eve. The three tiers of boxes were draped in rich red velvet, and on the walls hung paintings of great Shakespearian actors.

Many New York stars performed at the Metropolitan, including, of course, Edwin Booth, who wouldn't miss a chance to come to the city that showered him with gold.

Four years after it was built, the Metropolitan burned to the ground. It happened to be a night when there was no performance so no one was hurt. Plans for rebuilding were made at once, and

The people of San Francisco flocked to the theater.

again there was a Metropolitan Theater, more extravagantly furnished than before.

It wasn't until the late sixties, when William Ralston built the California Theater, that the Metropolitan took second place. The theater was Ralston's pride, and he delighted in taking guests to performances there after a large dinner at a French restaurant.

The same Edwin Booth came to play his Shakespearian roles and found it easy to perform *Richard III*, *Macbeth* and *Othello* on succeeding nights.

The celebrated English actress, Adelaide Neilson, was asked to come to the new theater and she came. Mr. Ralston was charmed with her performances, and he saw that her rooms at the Occidental Hotel were filled with fresh flowers each morning. She was given a sumptuous banquet when she was ready to return to England, and she was presented with a diamond necklace worth thousands of dollars.

Though he was vitally interested in the theater and his bank and his horses and estates, Mr. Ralston had time and energy to be interested in many other activities. Each day when the bank closed in the afternoon, Ralston's horse would be brought from the stables and he would ride off across the city to Black Point for his daily swim, whatever the weather.

The most ambitious of Mr. Ralston's ventures was the building of the famous Palace Hotel. He wanted it to be the largest hotel in the world and the most elegant. He was unable to manufacture the quality of carpets he wanted or enough of them, so he arranged for the firm of W. and J. Sloane, one of the largest furniture companies in the country, to establish a store in San Francisco and supply him with floor coverings.

He set up woolen mills to make blankets and foundries to make locks and hardware. He built a clock factory across the bay in Oakland to manufacture the kind of clocks he wanted in each room. Furniture factories, too, he established. All the furniture was made in his own factory from natural, beautifully finished woods. Even the tobacco he planned on selling in the lobby of the hotel was being raised in his fields near Gilroy. Another factory made the silk draperies for the whole hotel from Ralston's silkworms. In a city where water was always scarce, Ralston brought the water for the hotel from a reservoir beneath, a reservoir that held 630,000 gallons.

The hotel was to be seven stories high, and

when all the expenses were figured out, each story was to cost a million dollars. More conservative citizens shook their heads in amazement at this extravagance, but Ralston's admirers called him a wizard and cheered him on.

When the hotel was finished at last, it covered two acres. It was indeed one of the wonders of the world, and visitors were eager to stay in the hotel that had cost a million dollars a floor to build. Fancy carriages with their passengers drove through the wide portals to the inner Palm Court, paved with large squares of black and white marble. In each corner of the court was a wide brazier filled with warm, glowing coals. A massive crystal chandelier hung from the center of the domed glass roof that covered the court. All around it were balconies where lovely ladies in rich silks sat and watched the new arrivals in the court below. The scent of limes, oranges and lemons and other rare plants filled the warm air. In the Palm Court, too, were held the elegant balls; and night and day, orchestras filled the air with music.

Mr. Ralston was at the Palace Hotel almost as much as he was at his bank. He was prouder of the great, luxurious building that could house twelve hundred guests comfortably than he was of most of his other accomplishments. People called it Ralston's Fairy Palace.

When a man has made a very successful career for himself, he sometimes acquires enemies, even if he has been honest in his dealings. So it was with Ralston. The envious men began to whisper and start rumors. Some people, if prosperity wanes for them, find ways of blaming it on the man they envy. Mr. Ralston with all his success so far and his generosity to the city he loved so well, was in a position to be envied by men who hadn't been quite so successful and even some who had.

The silver kings of Nevada who lived in San Francisco were not so enthusiastic about Mr. Ralston as the rest of the people. They thought he was reckless, and they didn't like the way he was lending money to men who were building smaller mills in Nevada for mining silver. They decided to open another bank of their own in competition with the Bank of California that was getting so much of the Nevada silver. When the Bank of California heard about this, Mr. Ralston and his partner, William Sharon, issued new Bonanza stocks and the Bonanza crowd fought back.

This caused a financial panic, and the Bank of California had to close its doors on an August afternoon in 1875. On this afternoon after the bank was closed, Mr. Ralston went as usual to Black Point, put on his bathing suit and swam out into the choppy bay. This time the icy waters were too much for the tired banker and he drowned.

Nevertheless, the Bank of California opened its doors once more, headed by William Sharon, and the activities of Ralston's Palace Hotel went on as usual.

By 1876, though, the people of San Francisco became a bit uneasy. The wheat crops failed that year, and the large amounts of silver from Nevada that had come so regularly to San Francisco dwindled to almost nothing. The eastern market fell off for products of California, and shipping came to a standstill. There were unemployed men in large numbers in the city. Men were hungry for the first time, and they became angry and felt that they were unjustly treated. Mobs tried to burn ship docks and the rail terminal. There were parades of people who wanted work. The old Vigilance Committee reorganized for a short time, calling itself the Committee of Safety.

Labor agitators appeared in the city, and they increased the feeling of discontent among the working people by their speeches. These men were called "sand-lot orators" and they stirred idle crowds by their speeches against the silver capitalists and the railroad barons. They held mass meetings in the vacant sand lots near the city hall.

The chief rabble rouser was Denis Kearney, an Irish drayman. He organized the Workingman's Party and told the crowds that all the capitalists should be strung up. He said the dreadful depression was due to their greediness for wealth. His phrases have been used by agitators all over the country since. He said, "Tax the rich so as to make great wealth impossible. Take the government from the rich and restore it to the people. Let bullets replace ballots." These dangerous phrases were repeated by the angry, restless workingmen up and down the steep hills of the city. When these angry threats didn't get the results Kearney expected, he fell on the familiar scapegoat that San Francisco had persecuted over six years before. The new slogan was "The Chinese Must Go." Kearney told the people that the Chinese with their cheap labor were taking the bread from the mouths of the American workingman.

Kearney even orated on Nob Hill where the millionaires lived. There the mobs shouted their angry phrases at what they called "the shoddy millionaires" who, they said, were responsible for bringing the Chinese to California in the first place. The crowds shouted, "Destroy the hell-hounds of California, blow up the steamship docks, hang the legislators. Let the rope be our battle cry!"

By this time the newly formed Committee of Safety was aroused to the dangers of all this intemperate shouting. No one was hanged, though, or shot. Men had calmed down somewhat since the last Vigilance Committee did its work in 1856.

At last the shouts boiled down to just one and it was "The Chinese Must Go." This finally resulted in the Chinese Exclusion Act, which prohibited Chinese immigration for a period of ten years but did not interfere with the Chinese already in the country. After the ten-year period, the law was made more stringent. The Chinese were still excluded, and the government was given the power to expel from the country any Chinese who had been smuggled in unlawfully.

There was great excitement around this time when it was whispered that a smart young Scot named Andrew S. Hallidie had a wonderful idea to operate cars by steel cable. Transportation was getting more and more difficult with so many new people, and most of them crowded near the center of the city. The cumbersome horsecars would get stuck in the heavy mud, and they were slow and uncertain.

Only the millionaires could afford to live on the high hills, with their saddle horses and fast carriages to take them up and down. If cars could climb the hills, anybody could build up high and see the ships sailing in and out of the Golden Gate or look across the bay on clear days to Oakland and Berkeley.

So all men were interested in young Hallidie's idea and wanted to put money into the manufacture of the new cable cars. He put twenty thousand dollars of his own money into the venture and accepted only what he needed as he went about the weaving of the cables in his small factory on Mason Street.

In 1873 he completed his first car and it was pulled by strong steel cables, laid underground, up and down Clay Street. Everybody wanted to ride the new car as it jerked its way up and down the steep hill. Then a group, headed by Leland Stanford, built a second cable line on California Street. By the end of the eighties the high places of the city were laced with the new cable lines, and the ground hummed as the fragile-looking, open cars climbed up and down the hills. The old-fashioned horsecars soon disappeared.

There were still flurries of excitement when someone told of a new rich vein of silver in Nevada or a rich pocket of gold found in the foothills. San Franciscans expected these flurries and excitements. They had had them from the beginning.

Everybody wanted to ride on the new cable cars.

But after Hallidie invented the cable cars and strung his cables up and down the steep hills, people began to lose the feeling of waiting for fortune to favor them with sudden wealth. They began to think of building permanent homes for themselves and their families. Now there were cable cars to take them over the hilly places away from the business section. There were boats, too, to take them to Oakland and Berkeley across the bay. In the East Bay there were good schools. Mills College was on the outskirts of Oakland, and in Berkeley there was the young University of California nestled among the oak trees.

Oakland had many factories where men could work for wages enough to support their families. Many men preferred this surer living to the sudden fortune that was not so sure.

The Chinese had properly taken their place in the city and lived above their shops where they sold the silks and jade that came from the Orient. Many of them still worked as servants for families in the city.

The state was becoming prosperous in a lasting way, but not from gold and silver so much as from the land and what it could produce. The water front was piled with great casks of wine from the Napa Valley and drums of olive oil from the olive groves near Sacramento. The great central valley shipped bales of grain and wool. The orchards of the Santa Clara Valley delivered tons of prunes to the city to be sent by ship and freight car to far points of the country.

The dream that the first mission fathers had for the land was at last coming true, over a hundred years later.

14 THE ALASKA GOLD RUSH

Toward the end of the Nineteenth Century San Francisco rated as one of the great cities of the world. Road companies made the long railway trip from New York to play in her many theaters, and whole opera companies came with their own costumes and stage equipment during the opera season. The young city attracted men of letters who came to work on its newspapers. Mark Twain had come earlier, had worked on the *Californian* and then had gone off to visit a miner friend, Steve Gillis, in the mining towns. Bret Harte, too, lived and worked in San Francisco. Robert Louis Stevenson had visited the city twice in his time. Senator George Hearst bought *The Examiner* for his young son, William Randolph Hearst. This was the paper that started the Hearst chain of newspapers across the country.

Shipping men saw the opportunities for vast trade with the Orient and established firms along the expanding water front.

Guided by an enterprising young man named Claus Spreckels, the Hawaiian Islands began to produce sugar. His ships made regular trips to the Hawaiian Islands as well as to the South Sea Islands and Australia.

Robert Dollar's shipping line ran ships up and down the Pacific coast, bringing lumber from the forests of Oregon. Later he developed a large trade with China and Japan.

When trade became slow in the middle nineties, there was another burst of excitement. News reached the city that there had been a tremendous gold strike in the Klondike region of Alaska. San Francisco suddenly seemed like the town of the California gold rush period. Men from all over the state hurried to San Francisco to outfit themselves for the new strike. Printers rushed to print pamphlets on how to manage dog sleds in the northern land, and sold them by the thousand to the new miners. Storekeepers hastily stocked their shelves with stout waterproof boots, fur-lined coats, canvas tents, and picks and shovels. The miners bought the new equipment and didn't hesitate to pay the high prices asked. Then they rushed off to get any kind of passage on the boats leaving every day for Alaska and the new gold.

By now the city was moving out over the flat sands toward the Pacific Ocean. Market Street started at the Ferry Building and ran in a straight line toward Twin Peaks.

The large sandy front, near the ocean, was being reclaimed and planted in fast-growing trees that would break the sweep of wind coming from the Pacific. This land was set aside for a park and the man who planned it and lived to see it developed was a Scotsman named John D. McLaren. The park was called Golden Gate Park.

Soon gold was pouring into the city from Alaska. Over two hundred millions in gold had been dug out of the frozen soil since the gold rush began, and it was still coming. By 1898 California was celebrating her own golden anniversary of the discovery of the glittering particles by James Marshall in Sutter's mill race at Coloma.

The Golden Jubilee was a state-wide rejoicing, and each town had its own celebration. San Francisco outdid herself. There the celebration lasted for a full week, and the town was packed with visitors. On the first day the parade, starting from the Palace Hotel in the morning, didn't disperse until three in the afternoon when the final float passed in review beyond Van Ness Avenue. The army and the navy with their bands led off, followed by floats displaying the latest in mining machinery. There were Wild West riders, cowboys, Indians dressed in fine regalia, pretty girls on flower-covered floats, bearded men in miners' costumes carrying picks and shovels over their shoulders. They were all there, returning the cheers of the crowd who jammed the sidewalks and waved from the windows along the line of march. At night there were balls and concerts and banquets. In the new Golden Gate Park competitions were held for the children, and then good picnic lunches were handed out.

For a whole week the city was filled with music. Strolling Gypsies sawed their violins, and full

In the Golden Jubilee parade there were bearded men in miners' costumes carrying picks and shovels.

orchestras played in pavilions while choral groups sang on street corners night and day.

On the last day of the celebration, people watched a sham battle at the presidio and then went to Central Park to see the Wild West show. That night was the final grand ball and concert.

The jubilee was no sooner over than the Miner's Fair opened. Again there was the long parade with whistles and shouts and rockets shot into the air.

People gathered in Woodward's Gardens for the music and speeches. The city school children formed a living, laughing flag below the speakers' platform, spreading out in broad rows of boys and girls in colored capes of red and white to form the stripes. The field was made of boys wearing capes of blue, and on the breast of each boy sparkled a silver star. The flag rippled over a bank of seats into a bower of ferns. The movements of the children made the flag seem alive, and it flashed as if it were fluttering in a breeze. The children sang a farewell to the jubilee and a welcome to the opening of the fair. When their songs were finished, President McKinley in Washington touched a button that sent an electric spark flying across the country. At his touch a bell in the pavilion in San Francisco began to toll. Fifty taps were given on the bell. One was for each year since Marshall had found the first gold at Sutter's mill.

In early April, which was an eventful month, San Francisco had a sharp earthquake. It began about midnight and lasted a full minute. Tall buildings swayed back and forth, and some visitors in the city rushed from their hotel rooms in their night clothes. Police reported that a few houses in the Mission District had crumbled, but no one was injured. When the visitors heard this, they refused to go back to their rooms but sent for their blankets and slept in the public square for the rest of the night.

The San Franciscans, who had felt the earth tremors before, were not alarmed. Some of them found themselves telling the visitors that earthquakes were a perfectly natural happening and there was nothing to fear. They talked to the visitors the way the Indians had explained the shaking sands to Anza's pilgrims 125 years before, when they had been afraid. This time, though, it was a bit different. Now there were tall buildings to topple, and people were crowded into small spaces where they couldn't easily get out.

That same year on the 24th of April, Spain declared war on the United States. This was the beginning of the Spanish-American War. In a few weeks American troops were sailing for the Philippines from the wharves of San Francisco, the first American boys to leave their country to fight on foreign shores.

The First California Regiment was quickly organized and ready to embark. There was the usual parade with the troops marching four abreast down Market Street, their burnished guns shining in the sun. Thousands of cheering citizens lined the street. When the soldiers reached lower Market Street, the crowd became so enthusiastic that they pressed into the ranks of the soldiers and marched along with the men, pelting them with flowers.

One woman took her husband-soldier's gun from him and slung it across her own shoulders, while he carried their baby high above his head. The crowd cheered so that the drum and bugle corps could hardly be heard above the din.

At last the soldiers got aboard *The City of Peking*, the ship that was to take them to Manila. The docks were packed with the cheering people until the ship raised anchor and headed for the Golden Gate. As it passed Alcatraz, the guns on the island boomed out a farewell salute, and the First California Regiment sailed out into the Pacific.

The war was a short one. All actual fighting had stopped by the middle of August. In December the peace treaty was signed, and the boys were home again. Spain's world supremacy had been dwindling for a hundred years, and finally it was dead.

15 A NEW CENTURY

The passing of the Nineteenth Century was celebrated in San Francisco with the city's usual carefree gaiety. Grand balls, concerts, fireworks, and
the booming of guns ushered in the Twentieth
Century. Later in January there was a severe earthquake shock. People awoke to find their floors covered with smashed crockery that had been knocked
from shelves and cupboards. The old St. Nicholas

Hotel, a flimsy building, was badly damaged. Some people thought the earthquakes were getting more severe and discussed the idea of moving out of the city.

The city leaders even listened to a Japanese scientist who told them that he had perfected an instrument that could forecast earthquakes. It was proposed by some that it would be a fine idea to install one of these machines on the Farallone Islands outside the Golden Gate. Then advance bulletins could be sent to the mainland, warning the inhabitants when an earthquake was coming. Some agreed that this was a fine idea, but no one came forward with a gift of money to purchase and install such an instrument. It was a good topic of conversation, though, and most men laughed at the idea and agreed that earthquake-proof buildings would be more sensible. A few pointed out that although there had been three or four shakes a year for the past hundred years, there had been recorded in that time only sixty deaths. Many more people had been killed by being run over by carriages or falling off bucking broncos. An earthquake was no more of a hazard.

So the carefree people went about their affairs, and the Japanese machine was forgotten. In 1900 more silver was found in Nevada and the spot was called Tonopah. It mushroomed overnight. Then gold was struck in another Nevada town, Gold-field. Money again poured into San Francisco, and men talked of little else.

There was the same fevered rushing about, gath-ering of mining equipment and the hasty trip up the Sacramento River, then by team or horseback and even on foot over the Sierra Nevada to the new mines.

Another kind of gold was bubbling from the ground in the southern part of California, too. Crude oil had been discovered in the 1880's. Now speculation in oil stocks was heavy in San Fran-cisco.

When the next earthquake hit the city on New Year's Day in 1905, men were uneasy. Some won-dered if they would have been wiser to raise the money and buy that machine from the Japanese scientist, Mr. Omori. After all, he asked only two thousand dollars for it.

Newspapers commented briefly about the quake, and one editorial quoted a college professor who called the recent shock a mild disturbance. "A geo-tectonic earthquake is a sort of tame variety which may chafe against its chains now and then but never really does any harm," said the professor.

Several times during that year the city trembled

mildly, but the people remembered the words of the college professor and tried to pay no attention to the restlessness under their feet.

During the next spring, in the first week of April, 1906, San Franciscans were shocked to hear that Mt. Vesuvius in Italy had begun to spout smoke and flame again. The papers said that the city of Naples might well be buried in ashes the way ancient Pompeii was. Thousands of people were reported homeless and leaving the city.

San Franciscans, especially the large Italian colony, immediately organized committees to help the unfortunate city in Italy. Benefits were given and people contributed generously.

Some people declared that they couldn't understand why people wanted to live so near an active volcano. They said the Neapolitans must surely be a foolish people to run such a risk.

16   THE FATEFUL MONTH

In April of 1906 the Metropolitan Opera Company came all the way to San Francisco from New York to perform in the Grand Opera House. All the famous singing stars came in special cars, bringing with them quantities of scenery and beautiful costumes. Never before had San Francisco had so many fine singers in the city at one time; singers who had given successful performances in London,

Paris and Rome, as well as New York, came west to perform.

The city was in a great state of excitement from the Italian quarter in North Beach to the fine mansions on Nob Hill. Months before, when they knew the opera company was coming, the ladies of fashion sent to New York and even to Paris for handsome gowns of silk and satin. They had dressmakers busy for weeks designing dresses of chiffon and fine silk for their young daughters. When the time grew near, they took from the bank vaults their fine jewels to wear during the two weeks the opera would be in San Francisco.

Most of the opera company stayed at the Palace Hotel because it was nearer the opera house than the other hotels and, too, because it was the most elegant hotel in the city.

During their stay the inner court of the hotel was filled with fresh flowers each day, and ferns in great brass jardinieres lined the walls. Chinese boys in stiff white coats and trousers and long black pigtails were always ready to carry the guests' parcels and run errands for them night and day.

Bizet's opera *Carmen* was given on the night of April 17th. The great ladies of fashion sat in the tier of boxes wearing so many jewels that they looked as if they had Fourth of July sparklers stuck in their pompadours, twinkling red, blue and green. About their throats were high dog-collars of large pearls and diamonds, and strings of diamonds and rubies flashed on the pearl-embroidered bodices of their satin gowns.

The old opera house looked like a garden with masses of pink and white fruit blossoms banked against the walls. The boxes were roped in garlands of roses and ferns.

The artists of the Metropolitan gave a stirring performance in the flower-scented hall, and the audience cheered and clapped. The stout Caruso never sang clearer, purer notes. He and the entire company came to the footlights for many encores.

After the opera, people hurried to their carriages and drove off to gay supper parties. Members of the opera were taken to the great houses on Nob Hill for midnight celebrations. The parties lasted well into the early morning.

That fateful morning, the eighteenth of April, a bit after five o'clock, when the great Italian tenor Enrico Caruso was sound asleep in the Palace Hotel, he was suddenly and rudely awakened. His wide bed slid across the room, banging the opposite wall, and then leaped into the air as if invisible hands were jerking it to the ceiling and then slamming it down on the floor. The floor, too, was moving and there were sounds of crashing walls. Clocks, vases, pictures fell to the floor and smashed to bits. The windows fell in with a splintering of glass. There was a deep rumbling, louder than thunder, and the crash of falling walls all over the hotel. The tenor leaped terrified from his bed and picked his way across the glass-strewn floor that was bucking like a wild horse. He flung open the door. In the hallways he found other members of the opera company in their night clothes, all pale with fright.

The singers hurried over the moving floor and made their way downstairs to the lobby. There were the other hotel guests, some still in their night clothes and others in ridiculous costumes. One man had on an opera hat and was wearing an overcoat over his nightshirt.

Caruso sat on a small trunk in the lobby with his head in his hands, shaking with fright. There was a moment of quiet and he rushed back to his room and put on slippers and a coat, grabbed a towel and wound it about his throat like a muffler. Then he saw a framed picture of President Theodore Roosevelt which the President had autographed to him, still standing on the lopsided dresser. He snatched this up and started off to the lobby again with the picture clutched to his chest.

Snatching up the picture, Caruso started downstairs.

In the lobby people huddled together not knowing what to do. Every minute or so the whole building would shake and furniture would topple. Finally one member said everyone must get out of the building before it came crashing down upon their heads. There was a rush for the out-of-doors, and the hotel guests picked their way out of the lobby and along the cluttered streets to Union Square, where at least no buildings could fall on them.

Caruso was weeping with fear and kept repeating that he must get out of the city. Another member of the company, Antonio Scotti, was hunting frantically for a wagon to take the company out of town. At last he found a man willing to take the ones who wanted to go for three hundred dollars. Caruso and some of the others rushed back to the hotel and packed their trunks. Caruso, with his trunks, and some of the other opera singers got in the wagon. They were driven to the edge of town over the torn-up streets. They slept that first night in someone's yard. The next day some of the company managed to get a boat to take them to Oakland. Policemen didn't want to let them leave, but Caruso showed them his autographed photograph from the President of the United States and talked so convincingly in his fine dramatic voice that at last the officers let him and his friends get on the launch. At the dock in Oakland the picture served again as a passport for the terrified tenor, and he was taken aboard a transcontinental train and in a few days reached New York. He swore to reporters there that never again would he come to San Francisco, and he added that he would much prefer living at the foot of Mt. Vesuvius in his native Italy.

Meanwhile, back in the city, the earthquake that had come with no warning had wrecked a great part of the city and killed many people. Within a few minutes after the first shock on the first day, sixteen fires had started in different sections of the city. The streets were filled with half-dressed, frightened people, who still didn't realize the greater danger to come. Sleepy children carried puppies and cats under their arms. Many held bird cages with squawking parrots or frightened canaries. Everyone walked aimlessly back and forth. The earthquake tremblings still came every few minutes. Cracks would open in the street, some wide enough to drive a horse through. Streetcar tracks lay twisted into spirals on top of the pavement. Some of the streetcars lay smashed on their sides by the twisted tracks.

People pointed out to one another the flames shooting up in different parts of the city. They grumbled and complained that the fire department was not putting out the fires.

Then the truth was passed along in the crowd. The firemen couldn't put out the fires. Water

The earthquake wrecked a great part of the city.

mains all over the city were broken. There was no water. The only thing the firemen could do was to use dynamite to stop the fire from spreading.

The first day of the earthquake was a beautiful, warm, sunny day in San Francisco. This was unusual in a city that always had at least early morning fog. The people sweltered in the heat from the spreading fires and from the warm sunshine.

In the North Beach quarter the Italians tore carpets from the floors and hung them over the fronts of buildings. Then they got on the roofs and poured buckets of wine over the carpets until they were soaking wet. Even this didn't save the buildings. Thousands of barrels of wine were used, but the houses burned anyway.

Before the city was completely cut off from communication with the rest of the country, one employee of the postal telegraph office, the only man on duty, performed an heroic act. No one knows his name or what became of him. Right after the first terrific shock, he tapped out this message over the wires: "There was an earthquake hit us at 5:13 this morning, wrecking several buildings and wrecking our offices. They are carting dead from the falling buildings. Fire all over town. There is no water and we lost our power. I'm going to get out of the office as we have a little shake every few minutes, and it's me for the simple life. R., San Francisco, 5:50 A.M."

"Mr. R." did go away because when the operator in New York got the message he pounded frantically at the telegraph key, but San Francisco was silent. The telegraph people in the East wondered if the San Francisco operator had gone crazy to tap out such a grim message. Then after a while the wire was alive again. This time it was the superintendent of the company who tapped out the message. His message was: "We're on the job again and are going to try and stick." Then the telegraph people knew that the horrible news that had come earlier was true. Messages continued to come at intervals. "They are carting the dead from the falling buildings. There are so many fires and no one to fight them. Our roof is wrecked but not the entire building."

The fire got nearer and nearer to the telegraph building. The operator reported that all the water mains had been destroyed. He reported that the sound of dynamite came regularly from the buildings that were being blown up to keep the fire from spreading. The brave operator was still at his post well after noon and his wire clicked the message to the waiting officials at the other end: "Fire still coming up Market Street. It's one block from the

Post Office now. Back to the Palace Hotel is a furnace. I'm afraid the Grand Hotel and the Palace, too, will go soon. California Street is on fire. Everything east of Montgomery Street and north of Market Street is on fire now."

There was a lull in the message tapping and then came feebly over the wire, "We are packing up our instruments. We are ready to run." There was silence for a few minutes and then the message, "Good-bye." At the end of an hour came the final message: "I'm back in the office, but they are dynamiting the building next door and I've got to get out."

This is the way the rest of the country got the news of the doomed city. In a few hours people all over the rest of the country were busy gathering food, blankets, clothes and other necessities for the people of San Francisco. They were loading ships and trains and starting them off toward the West.

All of that first morning the dazed people of the burning city climbed farther and farther up the steep hills. Hundreds of silent people sat in the gardens of the mansions of Nob Hill and watched the fire snaking its red path up the hills toward them. They saw the downtown section with its tall buildings a smoky ruin. The people prayed for rain or even the usual thick fog that blew in from the Pacific Ocean, but the sun glared stubbornly in a blue sky and hundreds of new fires spurted up as far as they could see. By noon Chinatown, with its flimsy buildings, had gone and the terrified Chinese, carrying their possessions on bamboo poles across their shoulders, joined the other people on the hills.

Volunteer fire fighters, with regular firemen, tried desperately to save the pride of the city, the Palace Hotel. Finally the reservoir that supplied water for the hotel gave out, and the fire fighters had to flee when the windows of Billy Ralston's Fairy Palace began shooting out flames and smoke.

By the time the fire was licking at the fine mansions of Nob Hill, martial law had been proclaimed by the mayor, and General Funston's soldiers were in command of the city. No one was allowed inside the houses that had been damaged. Stoves were made of bricks with a sheet of metal for a top, and people cooked their suppers on the sidewalk. That first night no one stayed indoors. They curled up in the parks and gardens all over the city for their restless sleep.

The second day they woke to a morning of stifling heat, with showers of sparks and embers falling around them. The sun was shining as boldly as it had the day before, but now it was veiled by a cloud of thick smoke.

The second night was even more fearsome than the first, in spite of the fact that most people had been moved out of the dangerous areas. Most of the city glowed like a monstrous angry demon, breathing out flames and smoke. The heavy booms of the dynamite kept up a constant deep thunder. The dynamiting, though, had been the savior of the section beyond Van Ness Avenue. By the second day the fire was finally stopped at that wide street. Still the people, being cut off from the rest of the world, were fearful of everything and some of them believed the most ridiculous rumors. They heard that the whole East Coast had been engulfed by a huge tidal wave. Then someone started the story that Chicago was in ruins, although no one knew whether it was from fire or water. The San Franciscans wondered if their catastrophe was milder than the others.

As usual in times of peril in San Francisco, a committee was formed. This group was called "The Committee of Fifty," and men of good calm judgment were the ones chosen to take charge of the confusion and near panic.

When word got to the people that there was a committee of good citizens to work with the soldiers, they became confident and even gay. The ones who had grumbled the most and had wanted to get out of the city as soon as it was possible, decided to stay. That night groups of friends gathered around pianos that had been saved from the flames, and the citizens had impromptu entertainment. There were songs and recitations on the sidewalks. People began to talk of how they would rebuild their houses to withstand any other earthquake that might come.

The tent cities in Golden Gate Park and in the public squares formed their own sub-committees, and the men went hunting for canvas and boards to make shelters for their families. There was no distinction between rich and poor in those days after the earthquake. All stood in long lines together to get their ration of food and clothing and water that were handed out by members of the committee. People shared with one another. They had to. The people who had money in the banks could not get at it and so everyone was in the same boat. The food and clothing that were given them were the same, whether they were sailors, Chinese, or fine ladies who had worn sparkling jewels the week before.

Camps of refugees mushroomed in all the parks

of the city, but still there were those people who made haste to leave as soon as the authorities gave them permission.

Down Market Street, where the bricks were still smoldering and the streetcar rails twisted by the fire, hordes made their way to the Ferry Building. They carried bundles of clothes and pushed baby carriages filled with household goods from their ruined houses. There the emergency relief corps met them.

The Southern Pacific carried passengers and their baggage free any place they wanted to go, wherever it happened to be. Most of the people just wanted to get across the bay to Oakland, Alameda or Berkeley. The ferryboats took them across to the other side and there, if they wanted to go to Eastern cities, the trains stood waiting to transport them free.

Fifty thousand people were sheltered in Oakland during the emergency, some of them to settle there permanently. Oakland's small Chinatown took in the Chinese by the thousand. In Berkeley, at the university, the large gymnasium was turned into a lodging house. Those who couldn't find room there were given warm blankets, and slept under the spreading oak trees on the campus.

Two weeks after the disaster an official death list was issued. At that time three hundred and fifty bodies had been recovered from the ruins. The dead were taken to the Mechanics Pavilion. Portsmouth Square, too, was used as a public morgue. Many were taken to the presidio. The soldiers were needed for other work, so the able-bodied citizens were compelled to take over the task of burying the dead. Men who protested were forced at the point of rifles to help dig long, deep trenches. Everyone was assigned a task.

People were not allowed to roam the streets after nightfall unless they could show a badge proving that they were on official business. The city had to be protected from the looters. Soldiers challenged anyone who was wandering after eight-thirty at night. In the first hours after the quake, everyone heard about the proclamation that the mayor had issued, which was: "The Federal troops, the members of the regular police force, and all special police officers have been authorized to kill any and all persons found engaged in looting or the commission of any other crime." In this way looting of homes and business houses was kept at a minimum.

The fires raged through Thursday, when finally water was pumped from the bay to quench the flames. By Friday small fires still burned, but the danger of their spreading further was past.

Men who owned automobiles lent them to the Red Cross for rescue work. Automobiles were almost the only way of getting about the city because all the power lines were down, and the power houses of the cable cars had burned.

The morning of the earthquake the Governor, from his offices in Sacramento, declared the next three days legal holidays, and then, at the end of that time, extended the time for thirty more days.

Although tens of thousands of people had left the city by the end of ten days, there were still thousands left who were trying to get along in their temporary dwellings and who were thinking about plans for rebuilding their shattered homes. With the danger of more fires gone, San Franciscans regained their old confidence. The ones whose houses still stood moved back into them. The others, who were camping in Golden Gate Park and Portsmouth Square, fixed up their canvas and board houses with chairs, tables, pictures and ornaments that they had been able to save. Now it became an adventure to camp out in parks in the mild April weather.

One night after a welcome drizzle of rain during the day, a piano tinkled in Golden Gate Park. It was nearly ten o'clock, but the gay music brought fathers and mothers and children from their tents to listen to the music.

Campfires gleamed through the bushes, and the refugees brought their blankets and sat around the fire.

A laughing, red-headed boy sat on an upturned box at the piano and played "Home Was Never Like This." The people sang and clapped as he banged out the familiar tunes: "In the Good Old Summer Time" and "Dixie." The sleepy birds flew out of the trees, protesting in wild chirps, but the musician went on playing and singing with the campers, who for the moment had forgotten that their city was rubble and ashes.

17   SAN FRANCISCO REBUILDS
AFTER THE DISASTER

Only six days after San Francisco had been torn apart by the earthquake, and while buildings were still smoldering, a committee of leading citizens met in Mayor Eugene Schmitz's office to discuss plans for rebuilding the city.

Men whose great fortunes had been lost in the disaster were the first to make suggestions, and their enthusiasm gave courage to the downhearted.

159

William H. Crocker, the nephew of Charles Crocker, one of the founders of the Central Pacific Railroad, had lost a large fortune in the fire, yet he was one of the first to make a statement to the people of the city. He said, "Mark my words, San Francisco will arise from these ashes a greater and more beautiful city than ever."

And Darius Ogden Mills, who lived in New York but who owned great areas in San Francisco, was confident of the stricken city's future, too. "We will go ahead," he said, "and build the city, and build it so that earthquakes will not shake it down and fire will not destroy it, and we will have a water system that will enable us to draw water from the sea for extinguishing fires."

On April 20th, two days after the earthquake, Congress agreed to replace all the government buildings that had been destroyed and to repair the ones that were only damaged.

Although most of the newspaper plants had been destroyed, the papers were still printed daily across the bay in Oakland. Within twenty-four hours after the word of the San Francisco disaster got to the rest of the country, relief trains were on their way west. No one went hungry or thirsty for even a day.

The talk of rebuilding the city quickly with steel

At once people went to work to help rebuild the city.

reinforced buildings to resist future earthquakes did much to put spirit in the people.

Everyone went to work with enthusiasm. Rich men, who had been driving their automobiles or their fine carriages the week before, put on overalls and flannel shirts and got themselves picks and shovels. The city had to be cleaned up before any building could be done.

Makeshift shops opened on Van Ness Avenue, and soon ladies were looking at the pretty silk dresses on the shelves. Restaurants opened once more, and there were dances held on hastily constructed platforms. Everyone worked hard during the day; but at night the city still had the carefree, happy spirit that it had in the prosperous days of the gold rush.

Most insurance companies paid off on the burned property. The money in the bank vaults was in circulation once more, and the United States Treasury deposited ten million dollars to the credit of the local banks. Financiers all over the country offered to lend money for new construction.

The people were grateful and confident and went to work with spirit. The cleaning up of the city took months, and by December of 1906 some of the new earthquake-proof buildings had been started.

Three years later the city got a report that New Orleans was being considered as the site for an exposition to celebrate the opening of the Panama Canal, linking the East with the West. The citizens were indignant. Why should New Orleans have that distinction? San Francisco was the logical place for the exposition. Hadn't a great many of her citizens crossed Panama for the gold fields when they had to tear their way through an almost impassible jungle? Never, they said, would they allow New Orleans to have the celebration.

Although San Francisco was only partly rebuilt, a mass meeting was called, and thousands of citizens trudged through the still cluttered streets to attend. It took just two hours for four million dollars to be pledged for the exposition fund.

Five years later, San Francisco celebrated the opening of the Panama Canal linking the Atlantic and Pacific oceans, by throwing open the gates of the Panama Pacific International Exposition.

Meanwhile World War I had begun in Europe. Some men in the rest of the country predicted that the great San Francisco exposition would be a failure and that people would be too troubled to attend a "Fair" however grand it was.

Perhaps these men didn't know the spirit of San Francisco, for their predictions did not come true. Men, women and children flocked to see the exposition from all corners of the two Americas as well as from Europe and the Orient. Most countries had exhibits in the famous palaces that dotted the three hundred acres of land on the water front of the bay. Famous artists, artisans and architects planned the walled city within a city. Engineers built lagoons, and landscape artists bordered them with palms and exotic shrubs and flowers, and massed beautiful plants and trees in the courtyards. The buildings which housed the exhibits were actually replicas of Oriental and European palaces, with domed ceilings in sky blue, and pointed minarets. They shaded in warm sunset colors from the palest pink to a vivid orange.

For a whole year the fair was crowded with visitors. When at last it closed its doors, America was soberly wondering if she too would be involved in the war that was raging in Europe. In 1917 it happened. America was at war, and San Francisco, remembering her fine carefree year of the exposition with sadness, prepared recruiting camps for soldiers, and readied the port for wartime shipping.

During the year and a half of the war, shipbuilding expanded in south San Francisco as well as across the bay in Oakland, Alameda and Richmond. Workers flocked here from other parts of the country to work in the war plants.

When the war ended in November, 1918, most of these people decided to stay on and build homes in the San Francisco Bay area, where wages were good, and everyday living was more pleasant than in the less temperate parts of the country. These men found a great variety of employment in the nine counties surrounding the city and fine opportunities for their children to attend good schools and colleges. All these factors helped them to decide to live in the area.

As far back as 1856 there had been talk among the city fathers of a bridge that would span the waters of the bay connecting San Francisco and the cities of Oakland, Alameda and Berkeley. The ferryboats had a regular schedule to these cities, but men were thinking of a faster means of transportation.

Plans were being discussed. Finally in 1933 they were complete, and work began on the East Bay Bridge. Just three years later the bridge was completed. In November, 1936, it was open to traffic.

The bridge is really two bridges, each span starting out from opposite shores and meeting at Yerba Buena Island in the middle of the bay. For many years this wooded island, owned by the United States government and used as a naval training station, was called "Goat Island." Now everyone uses the old name, Yerba Buena.

The East Bay Bridge is the largest bridge in the world, measuring over eight miles in length. It has two decks. The top deck accommodates six lanes of automobiles while the lower deck takes large commercial trucks and the commuting trains. The cables and pillars of this long graceful bridge are painted a silvery gray.

Golden Gate Bridge swings across San Francisco Bay.

The following year San Francisco completed another bay crossing. This is the Golden Gate Bridge. It is a beautiful suspension bridge that joins the city to lovely Marin County on the north. It is a mass of heavy steel cables like a giant web and swings across the rushing, hazardous waters of the Golden Gate, the waters that took the lives of so many early navigators. This single span, the longest in the world, is an awesome sight. Its heavy cables painted a vibrant orange seem to sing in the wind that constantly blows between the two cliffs supporting its heavy piers.

The East Bay Bridge links San Francisco with its sister cities of Oakland, Berkeley, Alameda and Richmond, and the rich inland valleys. The Golden Gate Bridge brings closer to the port the tremendous redwood empire of the North. The resort area of the Russian River country is only a couple of hours by car. The fruit from the orchards of Sonoma County and the grapes from the famous Napa Valley can be transported easily to the city by truck. Too, there are the poultry farms of Petaluma that supply the city with quantities of eggs and chickens for the markets. The two great bridges succeeded in drawing all these communities together for the prosperity of all the people.

After the completion of the bridges, San Francisco began thinking about another world exposition, despite rumblings of war once again in the Orient and Europe. New York was to have an exposition in 1939. San Franciscans decided that the West Coast metropolis should have one too and immediately began laying plans. The site of the 1915 exposition had been cut up into lots and was covered with homes, with a great boulevard running along the water front connecting with the Golden Gate Bridge. So the planners had to look elsewhere. After much consideration, it was decided to dredge enough sand from the bottom of the bay to build a four-hundred-acre exposition site alongside Yerba Buena Island in the middle of the bay. The new site would be called Treasure Island.

So in 1939 expositions opened simultaneously in New York and on Treasure Island in San Francisco Bay.

Treasure Island, lapped by the ever-changing waters of the bay, entertained over seventeen million visitors during the two years of 1939 and 1940.

When the exposition was finally over, the war threat to America was blacker than ever. All too soon came that dreadful day that stunned the world when, on the seventh of December, 1941, the Japanese dropped bombs on sleeping Pearl Harbor.

Since her earliest beginnings, San Francisco had felt that the Hawaiian Islands were almost a part of her mainland. In the gold rush days, she remembered, the miners even sent their washing to Honolulu to be done. The Kanakas had come back and forth regularly to San Francisco even when the city was a small village. In later years the young people of Hawaii came to the bay area to go to school and college, and the older people came to do their shopping once a year. Yes, San Francisco realized that this war was right on her doorstep.

In less than a week the city and the whole bay area was on a strict wartime basis. There was a brown-out every night; there were air-raid drills with complete blackouts. Improvised bomb shelters were set up and, most important of all, the whole embarcadero was made ready for shipping of men and goods to the Pacific war. Troop ships and cargo vessels, camouflaged in great patches of blue-green paint to blend with the Pacific waters, pushed their snub noses steadily through the rough currents beneath the wide orange span of the Golden Gate Bridge on their way to war. There was a constant hum of airplanes winging over the bridge from the international airport south of the city. Men worked twenty-four hours a day along the water front, loading mountains of cargo, the needed war material, food and clothing for our troops overseas. So San Francisco became one of the most vital ports in the whole country.

As the war progressed in the next few years, the city became such an important one in the world as well as our own country, that it was chosen in 1945 to be the seat of the conference to form the United Nations. In April of that year a meeting was called of leaders and statesmen from all the peace-loving countries of the world. This was one of the most significant meetings of our time, for at this conference the charter of the United Nations was written and adopted. The purposes of this famous charter are: "To maintain international peace and security . . . to develop friendly relations among nations based on respect for principles of equal rights and self-determination of peoples . . . to achieve international cooperation in solving international problems of an economic, social, cultural or humanitarian character . . . to be a center for harmonizing the actions of nations in the attainments of these common ends."

Six years later, in 1951, San Francisco was the setting for another conference when the final treaty between our country and Japan was signed.

The tremendous growth in industry and transportation still continued after the war ended in

1945. There was still much to be done. Troops and equipment had to be brought home from the Pacific, and war industry began reconverting to make goods for the civilian population which had done without many necessities during the war years. And once more men who had come from other parts of the country stayed on to work in the new industries and to settle with their families in San Francisco and the bay counties.

Some men in San Francisco suggested at this time that it was ridiculous to keep the clumsy cable cars that bumped and clanged up and down the steep hills. The city was too big for them. They suggested that this outmoded form of transportation should be replaced with modern buses.

Immediately a storm of protest arose from old San Franciscans, as well as from others in all parts of the country who had ridden the cable cars and loved them as a part of the city. There were arguments back and forth, and phone calls and letters deluged the Mayor's office.

One elderly man remembered how, when he was a small boy, a friendly "gripman" always helped him boost his Shetland pony aboard the car at the stable and let them both ride for a few blocks where the hill was too steep for the pony. One housewife asked indignantly how she could give up

riding on a cable car whose "gripman" obligingly
let her off right at her own doorstep in the middle
of the block, and even helped her carry the bundles
into her house. Others said they didn't care if the
cars were out of date, they loved them. They loved
the cool breezes that whipped their clothing about
them and made their faces tingle as they rode the
cable cars. They enjoyed clutching the handholds
as the cars swung around the sharp curves. They all
agreed that riding on a cable car was far greater fun
than riding on a Ferris wheel and that the cars were
a very important part of the hilly city and must
stay.

So the sturdy little cars resembling plump, brown
and yellow bumblebees were kept. Now almost a
hundred years after Andrew Hallidie dreamed
them up, they still climb the steep hills of the city,
with an incessant clanging of bells, and cheerful
quips from the "gripman."

A visitor to San Francisco can take the Powell
Street cable and ride straight up Powell, with bells
clanging, to California Street. Getting off here
and walking one short but steep block up California, he will find the tall, modern Mark Hopkins
Hotel. It is on the site of the famous Nob Hill
residence of Mark Hopkins, one of the four Railroad Kings of the 1860's. Here the hotel elevator

shoots to the top of the building non-stop, to a large glass-enclosed room called "The Top Of The Mark."

At sunset on a clear day you can see for miles. Then to the northwest, the bright orange web of the Golden Gate Bridge is silhouetted against the blue sky. A bit to its left is the sun, like a ball of fire dropping rather fast beyond the deep blue mountain.

If there is no haze, the Farallone Islands stick their heads up from the ocean beyond the bridge like giant black seals. Below the bridge the fishing boats with gaily painted sails come dancing home over the choppy waters with their day's catch.

Toward the east, the Bay Bridge gleams like burnished steel in the afterglow. The steady streams of cars flash along the bridge like the changing colors in a kaleidoscope. The lights of the city begin to come on. In the business section the neon red and green and blue streaks flash importantly from tall buildings. Gradually over the hills for miles down the peninsula the whole city twinkles and winks like thousands of dancing fireflies. Soon the misty fog tunnels in through the Golden Gate and tosses a gauzy veil over the city. Finally the Top Of The Mark seems like a huge airplane hanging motionless, high in the air.

The little hamlet that began nearly two centuries ago with a population of just three hundred brave pioneers from Mexico has increased over the years to about 775,000 people while the population of the whole bay area has grown to nearly three million. The whole state has a little over eleven million people living within its boundaries. California itself is one of the great industrial centers of the nation.

It also has large gold-mining interests, lumber mills, cattle and sheep ranches. San Francisco is considered one of the finest shipping centers of the world, with its location close to the Orient and the Pacific islands, and its fine communication lines by air, rail and water.

California's greatest wealth, though, comes from the crops of her fertile valleys. The San Joaquin Valley, southeast of the bay, is two hundred and fifty miles long and fifty miles wide. It is the largest continuous block of cultivated land in the state, producing cotton, wheat and fruits of all kinds. The Sacramento Valley to the north is equally fruitful, while the reclaimed desert of the Imperial Valley in the south grows fruits and vegetables, and ships them all through the year to the markets of the whole country.

So, finally the wise words of Don Luis Peralta

spoken to his sons when the gold fever was spreading in the land have proved true. "Plant your lands and gather your crops." That is what California is doing today. That is her gold.

INDEX

177

LANDMARK BOOKS

★

Have you read these World Landmarks?

★

CHECK THE LIST BELOW

W-1   **The First Men in the World,** by Anne Terry White

W-2   **Alexander the Great,** by John Gunther

W-3   **The Adventures and Discoveries of Marco Polo,**
by Richard J. Walsh

W-4   **Joan of Arc,** by Nancy Wilson Ross

W-5   **King Arthur and His Knights,** by Mabel L. Robinson

W-6   **Mary, Queen of Scots,** by Emily Hahn

W-7   **Napoleon and the Battle of Waterloo,**
by Frances Winwar

W-8   **Royal Canadian Mounted Police,**
by Richard L. Neuberger

W-9   **The Man Who Changed China,** by Pearl S. Buck

W-10   **The Battle of Britain,** by Quentin Reynolds

W-11   **The Crusades,** by Anthony West

W-12   **Genghis Khan,** by Harold Lamb

W-13   **Queen Elizabeth and the Spanish Armada,**
by Frances Winwar

W-14   **Simon Bolivar,** by Arnold Whitridge

W-15   **The Slave Who Freed Haiti,** by Katharine Scherman

W-16   **The Story of Scotland Yard,** by Laurence Thompson

W-17   **The Life of Saint Patrick,** by Quentin Reynolds

W-18   **The Exploits of Xenophon,** by Geoffrey Household

W-19   **Captain Cook Explores the South Seas,**
by Armstrong Sperry

W-20   **Marie Antoinette,** by Bernadine Kielty

W-21   **Shakespeare and the Globe Theater,**
by Van H. Cartmell

W-22   **The French Foreign Legion,** by Wyatt Blassingame

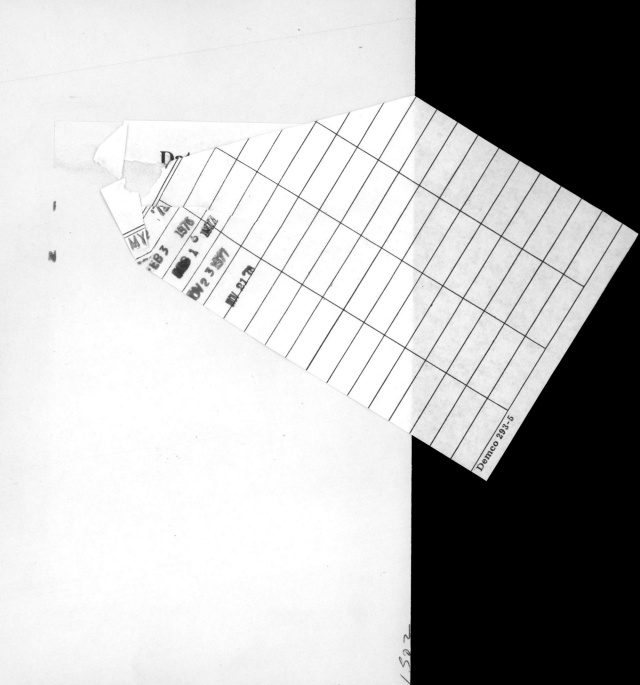